HOW TO WRITE A VERTICAL SERIES IN 10 DAYS

THE COMPLETE GUIDE OF MICRODRAMA STORYTELLING

ISABEL DRÉAN

WITH OCTAVIA MCKENZIE

CONTENTS

Issued in print and electronic formats.

ISBN [979-8-9939571-0-4] (paperback)

ISBN [979-8-9939571-1-1] (ebook)

Editor: Octavia McKenzie

INTRODUCTION
THE VERTICAL
REVOLUTION

My journey in storytelling began long before vertical series existed. I started out as an actress in Montreal, then moved to New York City in the 1990s to study theater at the Lee Strasberg Institute. By twenty-three I had produced my first Off-Broadway play and launched a small theatre company—but by the year 2000, I felt a pull to leave everything behind. I wanted to see the world.

That journey led me to Laos, where my life took an entirely unexpected turn. I became the first person to bring books into the country after the communist era, opening a bookstore and tea room that I would run for the next ten years. Twenty-four years later, I am still the proud owner of L'Étranger, Books & Tea in Luang Prabang. During that time I also launched the most popular bar in Laos, created a fair-trade company, and commercialized bamboo straws—this was 2002, long before sustainability became a movement. In 2008, I won the Sundance Channel's Grand Prize for The Best Green Idea.

But by 2010, the dream of making films had returned.

I moved back to Montreal with an idea I had first imagined in 1999: a curated platform for independent short-form content. When I came home, no one had built anything like it, so my partner at the time and I created it ourselves. On August 31, 2010, we launched KEBWEB.TV, the first indie web series streaming platform. Over the next five years we developed more than forty series. I produced and directed a web series titled *Manigances*, which won awards internationally, including the Grand Prize at LA Webfest. We sold the show to a Canadian TV channel, secured distribution, and eventually sold it to a major studio in my first pitch to Hollywood. It never got made—which happens—but it launched my career.

I moved to Los Angeles with my two young children. My directing dreams proved impossible as a single mother, so I turned to screenwriting. I rewrote a psychological thriller I had originally written with my mother back in 1999, and within three months it placed in the Quarterfinals of the Academy Nicholl Fellowship. I took it as a sign that I could do this. I spent the next few years mastering the craft, although without much success at first.

Everything changed at the end of 2019.

A producer I had developed a pilot with asked if I would write a Christmas movie. At the time I was focused on horror and thrillers— I barely knew anything about holiday romances. But I studied them, watched dozens, and developed a new process to write faster and stronger first drafts. It worked. Over the next eighteen months, five of my scripts went into production: *Secret Santa*, *Christmas Beneath the Stars*, *Christmas on the Rocks*, *An Eclectic Christmas*, and *The Holiday Swap*.

After years of struggling, I realized the holiday space was more accessible than the markets I had been chasing. I wanted others to have the same opportunity. I began mentoring writers and became deeply committed to helping them break in.

Which brings me to the spring of 2025, when my friend Sid Zanforlin asked if I wanted to write a vertical series.

I had never heard the term. He explained that the company he was working with wanted a professional writer who could bring a more female-empowered voice to their projects. I took the meeting, got the job, and immediately began studying the format—watching everything I could find. My first vertical series was an adaptation of a Chinese property. I wrote it fast and it paid the bills, but I could not ignore the massive opportunity unfolding in front of me.

The producers were happy. They hired me again to write an original project titled *Blind Desire*. They gave me a concept; I wrote what became THE BLIND BRIDE OF THE SCARRED MAFIA BOSS, which launched in October 2025 and climbed to number one on VIGLOO. It was still trending as this book went to print in December 2025. The other series I wrote will unfortunately never be released due to a chaotic production, but the experience opened a door I had not expected.

I was hooked.

The industry conversation shifted overnight: new apps, new companies, new money, new business models. Writers from my incubator were getting optioned and going into production for major apps.

The pace felt like a bullet train. Innovation everywhere. Hollywood struggling to adapt. AI rising. The entire landscape changing. I became convinced that the only way for creators to stay relevant is to learn, adapt, and ride the wave of change.

Vertical storytelling is not a trend. It is a global shift. The opportunities for writers are vast.

My hope is that this book gives you the tools to enter this world with confidence. Whether you want to write romance, thrillers, horror, fantasy, comedy, or something entirely new, there is room for you. There is need for you. There is opportunity for you. Verticals allow you to build a portfolio at high speed—to get produced, to strengthen your craft, to access opportunities that may be closed in traditional Hollywood.

This is your moment. The window is open right now, and I want you to step through it.

Let's begin.

Welcome to vertical storytelling.

Isabel Dréan

Los Angeles, December 2025

CHAPTER 1
THE V WORD

DOPAMINE ON DEMAND

WHAT IS A VERTICAL SERIES?

People watch everything on their phones now. On the bus, in line for coffee, during a lunch break, late at night under the covers. And almost always, they're holding the phone vertically. Vertical dramas are the natural evolution of how people already consume content: Soap operas on the go, built for a scrolling audience, told in 1–2 minute episodes, usually 40–70 episodes total, each ending on a cliffhanger.

The audience isn't looking for glossy prestige television. They want raw story, big emotion, high stakes, and characters who feel real and messy. They want drama that hits fast and keeps them hooked. These microdramas are addictive for a reason: They combine speed, tension, and emotional payoff with a structure that never lets the viewer rest. Viewers binge entire series in one sitting. And many viewers watch without sound. This means your characters, your images, and your emotional beats must be so clear that the story still lands.

Vertical dramas are not subtle. They are heightened, soapy, romantic, dangerous, melodramatic, and irresistibly fast. If you write a vertical drama with a killer hook, you can absolutely sell it. You don't need an agent or a manager. You don't need to live in Los Angeles. There is no barrier between you and production. This space is wide open.

SEE IT THROUGH THE VIEWER'S EXPERIENCE

Imagine you're scrolling TikTok. A dramatic moment pops up. Someone confesses a secret. Someone gets caught in a lie. Someone leans in to kiss. Then it cuts. Swipe up for the next episode. You swipe. Another twist. Another reveal. Another emotional hit. Before you realize it, you've watched twenty episodes. You hit the paywall. And you pay. Millions of people do this every single day. That is the vertical drama experience: momentum, emotion, cliffhangers, compulsion.

WHY VERTICAL DRAMAS HIT DIFFERENT

Verticals take everything you know about television pacing and compress it. There is no slow burn, no long setup, no filler. The story starts immediately and escalates every 90 seconds. Each episode delivers:

- One emotional beat
- One twist
- One reveal
- One cliffhanger

Viewers don't have patience for warm-ups. They want dopamine on demand. And if your story slows down? They swipe away. This is why mastery of pacing is everything. It's its own craft, as real and challenging as any other form of screenwriting, just built for a different ecosystem.

WHAT VERTICAL DRAMAS LOOK LIKE

Popular themes include:

- Soapy romance
- Women in peril
- Thrillers
- Crime and dark secrets
- Fantasy
- Revenge
- Money fantasy
- Young love
- Over-the-top melodrama

Think: Marriage contracts, hidden identities, double lives, blackmail, forbidden love, a billionaire with a dangerous secret, revenge arcs, and shocking betrayals.

Titles often feel like clickbait, on purpose.

You're writing for an audience that swipes, but will pay if the hook is strong enough.

HOW TO WRITE THEM

- Vertical screenplays are lean and streamlined.
- Short action lines
- Minimal blocking
- Every scene advances the plot
- Every beat builds toward the cliffhanger
- No more than 4 core characters (6–10 total)
- Average script length: 70–75 pages
- Voice overs are common because they clarify emotional stakes instantly.

Your job is to write addiction: Curiosity, compulsion, emotional impact in under two minutes.

Ask yourself constantly:

- What changes for my characters this episode?
- What is the twist?
- What secret is revealed?
- What question will make the viewer swipe to the next?

If you deliver that, producers will hire you again and again. And don't worry, we'll break down every one of these elements in the next chapters.

THE VERTICAL APP BUSINESS MODEL

Here's how vertical apps make money, and why this format is exploding. Apps like ReelShort, DramaBox, Vigloo, CandyJar, MyDrama, FlexTV, and GoodShort offer the first 10 episodes for free. After that, viewers can:

- Buy coins to unlock episodes
- Subscribe monthly
- Watch ads

Most viewers end up spending $50–$80 per month on a single series, roughly the length of a feature film. This is why these apps are scaling so fast:

- ReelShort made over $100 million in 2023
- DramaBox has over 90 million users
- In 2025, 1 in 5 entertainment apps worldwide were vertical drama platforms
- ReelShort plans to film 300 vertical series this year

The demand is massive, and the content volume is relentless.

THE AUDIENCE

Target audience: Women 25–54.

They want:

- Messy, lovable characters
- Emotional highs and lows
- Romance with danger
- Secrets, lies, and revelations
- Constant escalation

Some companies lean into problematic tropes. You don't have to.

You can write empowered characters, agency, consent, depth, and still deliver addictive, commercial storytelling.

Producers respect writers with a strong point of view.

TAKE ACTION: STEP 1

1. Download a few apps: ReelShort, DramaBox, Vigloo, CandyJar, MyDrama, FlexTV
2. Watch the first ten episodes of anything trending.
3. Study what hooks you, what makes you swipe, and what makes you pay.

Now you understand the ecosystem. Let's talk business.

CHAPTER 2
THE VERTICAL BUSINESS MODELS
SHOW ME THE MONEY

BEFORE WE GO DEEPER INTO CRAFT, WE NEED TO TALK HONESTLY ABOUT how this industry works. The current vertical boom rests on one foundation: The Chinese microdrama model. Fast production, extreme hooks, emotional intensity, and a paywall at the center of the experience. This system is proven, profitable, and expanding globally at a speed no one predicted. It is the blueprint Western markets are studying, copying, and adapting. But here is the truth writers entering this space must understand:

This is only the first business model. The industry is too new and too chaotic for anyone to assume this is the final shape of vertical storytelling. What we are watching now is only the beginning. To write verticals professionally, you need a clear picture of where things stand today and where the next opportunities are heading.

THE APP MODEL (THE ONE DOMINATING TODAY)

This is the model behind nearly every vertical app: ReelShort, DramaBox, AltaTV, Vigloo, CandyJar, MyDrama, and the hundreds more launching each year. Here is how it works.

Platforms commission production companies to create vertical dramas. They pay the full production fee. They keep all rights. They own the IP, the distribution, the audience, and the long-term revenue. Writers are paid upfront as work-for-hire. You write, deliver, get paid, and move on. No backend. No residuals. No ownership.

Why this model dominates

- Platforms already solved distribution through millions of daily users
- Monetization is proven through coins, subscriptions, and ads
- Marketing pipelines are built on massive social-video ad spend
- Production systems are fast and streamlined
- Risk is spread across dozens of monthly releases

Volume is the strategy. A single flop means nothing. Ten hits can transform an app into a global entertainment company.

What this means for writers

This model is perfect for writers who want credits, momentum, assignments, and consistent income. It is a path into the industry that does not require agents, managers, referrals, or Hollywood connections.

What you sacrifice is ownership, backend upside, and long-term revenue. Most of the money ends up with the apps. Writers and producers are paid upfront, while platforms retain all future upside. But here is the part most people overlook:

We do not know yet all the ways vertical series can be monetized or distributed. The app model is only the first version. Which brings us to the model now beginning to rise.

THE NEW FRONTIER: INDEPENDENT

This model flips the equation.

- Instead of the platform owning everything, creators retain rights and choose how to distribute.
- They may license a series to multiple apps.
- Release across social platforms.
- Partner with brands.
- Sell international rights.
- Or build a vertical channel of their own.

This model is early, messy, and still forming, but it is full of possibility.

Why this model is emerging

- The number of vertical apps is exploding, giving creators leverage
- Anyone producing elevated vertical content will immediately stand out
- Western audiences will eventually demand deeper, higher-quality stories
- Netflix, Amazon, Disney, and Fox are testing vertical formats
- Micro budgets make bold ideas possible for small producers
- Global distribution has never been easier

This model is not yet defined because it is still being invented. That is why it is exciting. The rules are not locked. The pathways are open. The ceiling has not been set.

Someone will define the independent vertical model. It could be a writer, a small studio, a collective, or an entrepreneur.

HOLLYWOOD IS MOVING IN

Something major is happening underneath the surface. Hollywood has entered the vertical space.

- Disney is developing vertical pipelines.
- Fox is investing in vertical-first studios.
- Netflix and Amazon are testing vertical formats worldwide.
- New companies like MicroCo and Gamma are building vertical frameworks from scratch.

When traditional entertainment giants enter a new format, they bring budgets, standards, infrastructure, and global distribution. They stabilize the industry. They elevate quality. They create prestige. Verticals will not remain low-budget or chaotic forever. They are evolving into a professional global storytelling medium. Writers who understand the format early will be the ones shaping what comes next.

THE MARKET TODAY: ASSIGNMENTS, NOT SPECS

Most of the work available right now comes from assignments. Production companies and apps already have ideas, prompts, or adaptations they want written. They hire writers to execute the vision, and the IP belongs to the company. You get paid for the script, not for the ownership.

Writers can pitch originals, but you should view a vertical spec as a sample first, a potential sale second. It proves you understand the structure, pacing, cliffhangers, and speed the space requires. A strong sample gets you hired.

Specs open doors. Assignments pay the bills.

This is the reality of the market today. The future will change, but if you are entering this space now, the quickest path to work is writing assignments and building a portfolio.

IP STRATEGY AND OWNERSHIP IN THE VERTICAL SPACE

Vertical series are **not a traditional spec market yet**. The majority of paid work today comes from assignments, where a company or platform brings the idea and the writer is hired to execute it. You are writing for a producer, not submitting a script hoping it sells. That means most opportunities in this space operate on **work for hire contracts**, with no backend or IP ownership retained by the writer.

This does not mean you should never create originals. It means you should be clear on how and when to use them.

Where Specs Fit Today

Specs are best used for:

- A writing sample (first 10 episodes) that proves you understand the format
- A project to pitch if you are willing to release ownership
- A portfolio piece to secure assignments, not necessarily to sell

Right now, a strong vertical spec script functions more like a **calling card** than an asset you expect to monetize directly.

When to Pitch an Original

Pitch when:

- You are open to selling the rights
- You are seeking work and exposure
- You would be happy to see the project made even without ownership
- The idea is designed for vertical structure, budget, and story engine

Pitching a spec can lead to paid assignments, contracts, and long-term relationships with producers. Many vertical careers start exactly this way.

When to Keep Your IP

Hold ownership when:

- The concept has franchise potential outside vertical
- You want to adapt it into a book, feature, or series later
- The idea is personally meaningful or brand defining
- You plan to produce it independently

If a story feels like your baby, protect it. You can always develop it as a vertical yourself or pitch it later when creator-owned models mature.

Why Ownership Matters

Selling IP means:

- You are paid once
- The company controls sequels, remakes, adaptations
- You do not participate in ongoing revenue

So be careful who you sell your babies to.

The Market Will Evolve

The current system favors platform-owned content, but that is only Phase One of this industry. The next wave will include:

- Creator-owned vertical IP
- Licensing and multi-platform distribution
- Cross-format adaptations (books, features, games, print)
- Fan-driven vertical brands and universes

We are early. The independent model will come. Being strategic today positions you to benefit tomorrow.

Simple takeaway:

Assignments grow your career today. IP builds your future tomorrow. Specs are your bridge between both.

THE BIGGER PICTURE

Let us zoom out.

We can all agree that the current business model, built on fast production and a paywall system, is the engine powering the vertical boom. But if people already watch most of their content on their phones, and we meet viewers exactly where their attention lives, then the audience for vertical storytelling is enormous.

This wave is not the peak. It is the beginning.

Verticals are not just a new format. They are a new storytelling ecosystem. A new business frontier. A new creative landscape waiting to be built.

We are not only adapting to a shifting industry. We are helping define its evolution. The opportunities will expand. The models will evolve. New players will enter. Entire approaches to distribution and financing will be invented.

As an entrepreneur and a storyteller, I find this thrilling. The possibilities are endless. This medium is far from finished growing. We are only seeing the tip of the iceberg. And you, stepping into this now, are early.

TAKE ACTION: STEP 2

1. Download several vertical drama apps and explore what is being made.

2. Notice the titles, the trends, the tropes, and the genres.

CHAPTER 3
WHAT WORKS AND WHAT DOES NOT
GIVE THE PEOPLE WHAT THEY WANT

THE VERTICAL SPACE MOVES FAST. TRENDS SHIFT MONTHLY. WHAT'S HOT today might be ice-cold in eight weeks. Romance dominates now, but horror, thriller, and branded comedy are breaking through.

One app releases a CEO romance every hour; another suddenly pivots to supernatural; a third posts its first comedy hit on TikTok.

I'm not going to predict what will be trending when you read this book. Anyone pretending to know is guessing.

But here's what *doesn't* change:

The psychology of why people binge vertical dramas. The way viewers swipe. The emotional patterns that trigger compulsive engagement. The structural beats that keep people paying past Episode 10. Those principles stay steady even as trends rotate.

This chapter gives you the foundational tools that work no matter the genre, market, app, or trend cycle. These are the mechanics behind vertical hits, the things producers look for and the things viewers respond to instantly.

THE FIRST 5 SECONDS RULE

You have less than five seconds to grab attention. If you don't hook them immediately, they swipe away. That's the reality of the format. Think of the very first image your viewer will see.

What is the moment that stops the scroll?

Strong openings include:

- A betrayal caught in real time
- A slap, a kiss, or a confession
- A pregnancy test
- A body on the floor
- A forbidden moment about to erupt
- A shocking reveal
- A character in danger
- A visual that feels dramatic, emotional, and heightened

Your opening shot is marketing. It's the ad for your story. It has to hit.

Ask yourself constantly:

- What is the strongest way to open this story visually?
- What would *you* stop scrolling for?

Start big. Bigger than you think. Then escalate from there.

WRITE TO YOUR GENRE'S EMOTIONAL ENGINE

Every genre has a core emotion. If you write to that emotion, your vertical drama will land.

Romance → Write from the heart.

- What gives *you* butterflies?
- What makes your chest ache?

- The audience must root for the couple. She can't be weak, and he can't be an irredeemable jerk.
- Love interests need chemistry, agency, and emotional momentum.

Thriller/Suspense → Write from your head.

- Be clever.
- Be calculated.
- Build tension like a mastermind.
- Every beat should raise the stakes or corner the protagonist.

Horror → Write from your gut.

- Fear has to be visceral.
- Visuals matter more than dialogue.
- Think dread, danger, shadows, vulnerability, and primal terror.

Vertical audiences respond to raw emotion, not subtlety. You are writing a heightened story. Embrace it.

CLIFFHANGERS ARE NOT OPTIONAL

Every episode must end with a reason to swipe.

The strongest cliffhangers are:

- **Revelations** ("I'm actually your sister…")
- **Interruptions** (the kiss that doesn't land)
- **Threats** ("If you tell anyone…")
- **Decisions** (stay or go, trust or leave)
- **Reversals** (everything they thought was true flips)

Your goal is to create an emotional inhale, not the exhale. Cut at the moment of escalation, not resolution. If your episode ends on a completed beat… you just killed the swipe.

EVERY 60–90 SECONDS, SOMETHING MUST SHIFT

This is where most writers fail. In vertical drama, every single episode must contain:

- a beat
- a reveal
- a twist
- a confrontation
- a decision
- a reversal
- a secret dropping
- a threat emerging
- a kiss landing or failing
- a hope rising or collapsing

If nothing changes, the audience feels it, and they swipe out. Vertical storytelling is not slow-burn. There are no long quiet moments. There is no space for reflection. The gear must shift constantly.

In this format:

- Momentum is the currency.
- Emotion is the engine.
- Change is the heartbeat.

WHAT DOESN'T WORK (SAVE YOURSELF THE PAIN)

These are format killers. Avoid them at all costs:

- **Slow burns:** Vertical audiences want heat fast.
- **Dialogue-heavy scenes:** No one is listening. Show it visually.
- **Complex world-building:** You don't have time for it. Keep it simple.
- **Ensemble casts:** Too many faces. Stick to 2–4 core characters, max 6–10 total.

- **Passive protagonists:** Your lead must make choices, not react endlessly.
- **Anything requiring deep concentration:** This is swipe-up entertainment, not prestige drama.
- **Talking heads:** Movement, escalation, and emotional clarity are mandatory.

THE BOTTOM LINE

Here is what always works in vertical storytelling:

- Strong visual openings
- Big emotions and immediate stakes
- Visual clarity over dialogue
- Cliffhangers every episode
- Active protagonists making choices
- Simple, clean concepts
- Constant forward momentum

And here is what doesn't work:

- Slow pacing
- Talk-heavy scenes
- Complex plotting
- Passive characters
- Subtlety or restraint

The format rewards clarity, emotion, and speed. It punishes hesitation, ambiguity, and intellectual distance.

Your job:

- Study what's working right now on the platforms.
- Absorb the patterns.
- Write boldly with your own voice.

TAKE ACTION: STEP 3

1. Watch five current vertical dramas in the genre you want to write.
2. As you watch, note:
   - What grabbed you in the first 5 seconds
   - What is the cliffhanger pattern
   - How are they using visual storytelling
   - What made you swipe
   - When your attention dropped and why
3. Do more of what works.
4. Avoid everything that slows momentum.
5. Case study to watch for this book: My #1 vertical series on Vigloo *"The Blind Bride of the Scarred Mafia Boss"*.

CHAPTER 4
WHY NOW IS THE MOMENT

IT'S THE WILD, WILD, WEST

RIGHT NOW, VERTICAL STORYTELLING IS IN A RARE PLACE, A MOMENT OF explosive growth, massive demand, and a shortage of writers who can actually deliver the format well. This creates something the traditional film and TV industry almost never offers:

A truly accessible entry point.

- "Not" accessible if you know the right people.
- "Not" accessible if you have representation.
- "Not" accessible if you went to film school.

Actually accessible.

If you can prove, with one strong sample, that you understand the vertical format, producers will hire you. This is not true anywhere else in the entertainment industry.

This chapter is about why this moment exists, what it means for you, and how to take advantage of it before the landscape shifts.

THE DEMAND IS OUTPACING THE TALENT POOL

Let's start with the clearest fact: Platforms and production companies cannot find enough writers who understand the format. Not enough writers know how to:

- Structure 40–70 micro-episodes
- Build compulsive cliffhangers
- Keep momentum every 60–90 seconds
- Write visually for a silent or half-silent audience
- Design big, immediate emotional stakes
- Deliver binge-worthy escalation

This year alone, thousands of vertical series will be produced across dozens of apps and international markets. Yet the hiring bottleneck is writers.

Producers say the same thing over and over again: "We can crew up. We can cast. We can shoot fast. We just can't find enough writers who get the format." That shortage is your opportunity.

THE QUALITY BAR IS STILL DEVELOPING

Let's be direct: Much of the vertical content being produced right now isn't great.

If you scroll through the major apps for an hour, you'll see:

- Flat cinematography
- Awkward pacing
- Weak performances
- Confusing episodic flow
- Clunky twists
- Little visual storytelling

This is not because platforms want bad content. It's because the format is new, the timelines are brutal, and the industry hasn't caught up yet. Even *competent* work stands out.

If you can deliver:

- Clear visuals
- Coherent emotional beats
- Consistent cliffhangers
- Characters with agency
- Simple, focused conflict

You are already ahead of most of what's out there. Competence currently reads as excellence. That window will eventually close, but it's still open now.

EVERYONE IS LEARNING IN REAL TIME

One of the biggest advantages of writing vertical series right now is that no one has decades of experience. There are no veterans with 20 years of vertical storytelling credits. There is no "established way" everyone must follow. The rules are being formed now, by the people actively doing the work. This creates a level playing field that does *not* exist in traditional Hollywood.

A writer with:

- Zero film school
- No agent
- No previous credits

You can genuinely compete with writers who've worked in TV or features for years, simply because no one is far ahead in this format. Newcomers are not behind here. They are arriving at the exact right moment.

YOUR SAMPLE IS YOUR CURRENCY

Here is the single most important fact about breaking into vertical writing: If you can write one strong sample that proves you understand the vertical format, you will get work. Not maybe. Not "if you know someone." You will get work. Producers skim vertical samples differently than traditional screenplays.

They look for:

- Does this writer know how to hook quickly
- Do they understand the pacing
- Can they escalate every episode
- Can they land a cliffhanger
- Can they write visually
- Can they keep it emotional and addictive

If the answer is yes, you'll get hired, often faster than you expect.

- This is not the reality in features.
- This is not the reality in television.
- This is not the reality in streaming.
- This is unique to vertical.

WHY NOW IS THE BEST TIME TO ENTER

You're entering during a moment when:

- The format is exploding
- The market is global
- The budgets are increasing
- Hollywood is paying attention
- New apps launch monthly
- International demand is massive
- The craft is still forming
- The talent pool is still thin

You can build a career here **before** the field becomes crowded and competitive. If you wait until the format matures, you'll be entering at the same time as the TV writers, the feature writers, the showrunners, the studio-backed creators, people with long résumés and built-in leverage.

Right now, the people being hired first are the people who understand the format first.

A REALISTIC WAY TO LOOK AT IT

You don't need to believe the hype. You don't need to assume the window will slam shut tomorrow. You don't need grand predictions.

Here's what you *can* rely on:

- The demand is real.
- The shortage of writers is real.
- The need for content is real.
- The pay is real. Not huge yet, but it is increasing.
- The opportunities are real.

And understanding the format gives you a meaningful, immediate advantage. This is the first time in decades that screenwriting has a genuine low-barrier entry point. Not because standards are low, but because the format is new. That combination never happens twice.

WHAT IT TAKES TO BE A VERTICAL WRITER

To thrive in vertical storytelling, you need:

- The kind of fire-in-the-belly drive indie filmmakers are made of.
- To enjoy the writing itself — the speed, the problem-solving, the rush of making scenes land in just a few lines.
- Grit, hustle, and the willingness to adapt on the spot.

- Fast pacing, flexibility, emotional clarity, visual instincts, and a love for constant momentum.

Vertical writers don't wait for inspiration; they create it. They learn the patterns, push the twists, embrace the chaos, and keep generating story no matter what's happening around them.

Do you think you have what it takes to become a vertical writer? Keep reading.

TAKE ACTION: STEP 4

1. Join a vertical series WhatsApp group or community.
2. Follow five vertical writers or producers on social media.
3. Start seeing what people are talking about in real time: the wins, the challenges, the trends, the opportunities.

This community is still small. Being part of it early matters.

CHAPTER 5
THE VERTICAL STRUCTURE

THE BLUEPRINT THAT NEVER FAILS

When writers first enter the vertical space, they often assume they need to erase everything they know about storytelling. You don't. Storytelling principles still apply. Character arcs still matter. Tension, momentum, emotional payoff, all the fundamentals are the same.

What changes is the rhythm.

Vertical storytelling compresses structure into small, high-impact units. The beats are tighter. Escalations happen faster. Cliffhangers are constant.

Instead of building toward three big act breaks, you're shaping a story arc across **dozens of short episodes**, each one designed to move the story forward and keep the audience swiping. You're not abandoning structure, you're adapting it to a format that demands immediacy, clarity, and momentum. Let's break down how that actually works.

THE FIRST 5 SECONDS RULE

In traditional screenwriting, you establish the "normal world" before disrupting it. In vertical, that entire step disappears. Your story begins at the disruption.

The inciting incident *is* your opening.

Not at minute five. Not at the midpoint of Episode 1. In the first five seconds. Drop the audience directly into tension, conflict, danger, desire, something they must understand immediately, visually, without dialogue. No warm-up. No backstory. No easing in. This is where most writers coming from film/TV struggle. Vertical storytelling simply doesn't allow for slow beginnings.

THE FIRST EPISODE: DROP US INTO THE STORY

At the end of Episode 1, your viewer should already know:

- Who the main characters are
- What the emotional or dramatic problem is
- What the stakes are
- The tone and promise of the entire series
- Why they want Episode 2 right now

If Episode 1 feels like "setup," it's already too slow.

THE FIRST 10 EPISODES: YOUR REAL SAMPLE

Before paywall. Before commitment. Before the viewer decides to invest. This is where platforms and producers decide whether your concept works. Producers ask for the first ten episodes because:

- They show your concept clearly
- They prove you understand the format
- They showcase pacing and escalation
- They demonstrate whether you can write cliffhangers

Episode 10 is the most important early episode. It's the "Act 1 break" of a vertical series. If Episode 10 isn't strong, the viewer doesn't swipe. If they don't swipe, they don't pay. If they don't pay, the platform doesn't buy more scripts. The entire business model hinges on this moment.

THE FUNCTION OF EPISODES 1-10

Here's what these episodes must do:

- Start with the inciting incident
- Establish the central relationship
- Show the core conflict
- Clarify the stakes
- Launch the story engine for the rest of the series
- Deliver a huge cliffhanger at Episode 10

Each episode delivers **one strong moment**, one twist, one emotional hit, one escalation.

They are short.

They are clean.

They are punchy.

They are addictive.

Your job is not to be subtle. Your job is to keep them swiping.

EPISODES 11-40+: ESCALATION, ESCALATION, ESCALATION

After the paywall, the viewer has committed. Now you deliver.

This section is no longer about introducing the story: it's about **escalating it**. Think in waves:

- Relationship deepens
- New obstacles appear
- Secrets surface
- Power shifts

- Betrayals land
- Choices intensify
- Momentum accelerates

Each episode shifts something. Small or big, but always forward. There is no "quiet middle." Vertical storytelling does not have that luxury. The middle is where most writers lose momentum. In vertical, momentum *is* the format. If nothing changes every 60–90 seconds, you lose them.

THE STRUCTURE IN SIMPLE TERMS

You can think of vertical structure like this:

- Episode 1: Inciting Incident (start in the fire)
- Episodes 2–3: Fallout + Decision
- Episodes 4–7: Escalation + Complications
- Episode 8–9: Crisis vs. Desire
- Episode 10: Mini-Climax + Massive Cliffhanger
- Episodes 11–40+: Rising stakes, revelations, relationship pressure
- Episodes 40–60+: Peak conflict, emotional payoff, resolution
- Final Episode: Satisfying ending (especially for romance)

This isn't a rigid template, it's a rhythm. A pulse. A way to keep the story alive through dozens of short episodes. It's structure in motion.

WHAT DOESN'T WORK IN VERTICAL STRUCTURE

- Slow builds
- Scenes with no shift
- Dialogue-heavy storytelling
- Episodic repetition
- Passive protagonists
- "Talking heads"
- Episodes that feel like filler

- Complicated world-building that needs explanation

If the episode feels skippable, the viewer *will* skip. If they skip too many, they stop.

YOUR JOB AS A VERTICAL STORYTELLER

You are creating:

- Emotional momentum
- Visual clarity
- Constant forward motion
- Big feelings in small packages
- Characters the viewer wants to follow
- Problems that escalate rapidly
- Cliffhangers that force the swipe

Vertical writing is not a lesser craft. It's a different craft, faster, tighter, more distilled. It rewards writers who can move story efficiently without losing heart or emotion.

TAKE ACTION: STEP 5

1. Choose three vertical dramas in your genre.
2. Watch the first ten episodes of each.
3. Write down:
   - How they open
   - What the hook is
   - How many characters are introduced
   - What Episode 10 cliffhanger is
   - What keeps you swiping
   - What made you lose interest
   - And what you would do better

This is your foundation. You can't write verticals if you don't study them.

CHAPTER 6
CREATE A MONEY-MAKING VERTICAL CONCEPT

MAKE YOUR IDEA THE EASIEST "YES" THEY'LL SAY ALL WEEK

BEFORE YOU WRITE A SINGLE PAGE, YOU NEED A CONCEPT THAT WORKS commercially. Not every idea translates to vertical. Some concepts seem great but can't sustain 40–70 episodes. Others look simple but generate endless complications. A vertical concept must be both **creative** and **commercial**. Without that combination, the series falls apart.

Here's what makes a vertical concept viable:

- **High-stakes central conflict**: Not subtle. Not slow. Not philosophical. The conflict must be immediate, clear, and massive.
- **Built-in romantic or dangerous tension**: It must generate chemistry or danger in every episode.
- **Clear visual storytelling**: Can be shown, not explained. Many viewers watch without sound.
- **Recognizable genres/tropes**: Audiences choose vertical stories based on tropes. Deliver them.
- **Binge-worthy setup**: Every episode creates momentum into the next.

- **Producible on micro-budget**: Small cast. Limited locations. High emotional spectacle, not expensive spectacle.
- **Broad emotional appeal**: Love, revenge, justice, ambition, belonging, fear, the universal drivers.

If your concept doesn't check most boxes, rethink it now.

THE CONCEPT BUILDING PROCESS

STEP 1: CHOOSE YOUR GENRE

Pick **one** primary genre. You can add a secondary for flavor.

Examples:

- Romance–Thriller
- Horror–Romance
- Thriller–Revenge

STEP 2: CHOOSE YOUR TROPES

Every successful vertical series uses **2–4 proven tropes**.

Tropes aren't clichés, they're promises.

Romance Tropes

- Contract Marriage
- Enemies to Lovers
- Secret Baby
- Billionaire CEO
- Forced Proximity
- Forbidden Love

Thriller Tropes

- Hidden Identity
- Revenge
- Witness Protection
- Corporate Espionage
- Double Life

Melodrama Tropes

- Long-Lost Heiress
- Family Rivalry
- Arranged Marriage
- Secret Past
- Hidden Pregnancy

Pick 2–4 that naturally generate conflict.

STEP 3: ADD YOUR HOOK

This is where generic becomes addictive.

Generic: Contract marriage revenge story.

Hook: She's blind, but secretly an assassin.

Generic: Billionaire romance.

Hook: She's a con artist scamming billionaires, until he catches her.

Your hook answers:

- What secret changes everything?
- What twist makes this version fresh?
- What gives the story endless complications?

STEP 4: TEST FOR COMMERCIAL VIABILITY

These five questions will save you months of wasted writing:

1. Can you shoot it in 3–6 locations?

Mansion, office, apartment, a café, perfect. Ten countries and time portals, no.

2. Can you do it with 6–10 actors?

Leads + family + antagonist = ideal.

3. Does it generate 40–70 episodes of conflict?

If it runs out after one twist, it's not viable.

4. Is it binge-worthy?

Every episode must create momentum.

5. Does it fit a proven vertical genre?

Romance, thriller, horror, melodrama: yes. Art film meditation on grief: no.

If you answer **YES** to all five, you have a commercial concept.

CONCEPT DEVELOPMENT IN ACTION

Example 1: Generic to Commercial

Starting Point: Romance. Billionaire + Contract Marriage.

Problem: Done a million times.

Hook: She marries him as part of a long-planned revenge plot, because she believes he killed her brother.

Commercial Test:

- Locations? Yes.
- Cast? Yes.
- 40–70 episodes? Yes.
- Binge-worthy? Absolutely.
- Proven market? 100 percent.

Result: Commercial vertical concept.

Example 2: Looks Good, Won't Work

Starting Point: Sci-Fi Romance. Time Travel.

Hook: Every time she saves him, someone else dies.

Commercial Test:

- Locations? No (multiple time periods).
- Cast? Maybe.
- 40–70 episodes? Risky.
- Market? Not proven.

Result: Better suited for a feature or novel.

WHAT YOUR CONCEPT MUST PROMISE

External Conflict (examples):

- Criminal threats
- Family pressure
- Corporate danger
- Class divide

Internal Conflict (examples):

- Secrets
- Attraction versus logic
- Moral dilemmas
- Trauma
- Loyalty versus self-interest

Escalating Stakes:

Someone's reputation, life, or future is on the line.

If your concept naturally generates conflict at all three levels, it's built for microdrama.

THE CONCEPT CHECKLIST

Before you commit, confirm:

- One-sentence concept
- Visual scenes pop immediately
- At least ten complications
- Three to six locations
- Six to ten characters
- Works for forty to seventy episodes
- Fits a proven genre
- Hook is distinctive
- You would watch it yourself

If NO to more than two items, keep developing.

YOUR CONCEPT IS YOUR FOUNDATION

A strong concept makes writing the series exciting. A weak concept makes every episode painful.

Spend time here. This is where most writers fail, and where you'll stand out.

TAKE ACTION: STEP 6

1. Pick one primary genre
2. Choose two to four tropes
3. Add your hook
4. Run the commercial test
5. Write it all down
6. Choose your best idea

This is your blueprint.

CHAPTER 7
THE CLICKBAIT TITLE

MAKE THEM STOP IN THEIR TRACKS

Your first opportunity to grab your audience's attention. Your title is your first pitch. If the title doesn't grab the producer, they won't read your logline.

If it doesn't grab the viewer, they won't click the series. In vertical storytelling, the title *is* marketing. It must promise drama, conflict, stakes, and secrets, instantly. A good title sells your entire concept in six to ten words.

MAKE IT PERSONAL

Add intimacy. Make it feel like a confession.

Instead of: **The Hot Alpha Billionaire**

Try: **My Hot Alpha Billionaire**

The possessive "my" immediately pulls the viewer inside the drama. It creates emotional ownership. It makes the story feel personal.

Possession = tension = clicks.

LENGTH MATTERS

In vertical, a one-word title is almost always too vague. Your viewer decides in seconds.

Your title must tell the audience:

- What kind of story it is
- Who it's about
- What the dynamic is
- What the tension is

Your title should work like a **mini-logline**, revealing conflict, stakes, or a secret.

INCORPORATE THE TROPE INTO THE TITLE

This is one of the most powerful shortcuts in vertical storytelling. Your title shouldn't just communicate the hook, it should tell the audience **exactly what trope they're about to get.** Tropes are emotional promises.

Examples:

- Enemies-to-lovers
- Forbidden love
- Accidental marriage
- Secret baby
- Hidden identity
- Forced proximity
- Arranged marriage
- Revenge romance
- Billionaire obsession
- Mistaken identity
- Rejected mate

Viewers tap based on tropes. If they love the trope, they click immediately.

You can signal the trope directly in the title by using:

- The relationship (Wife, Bride, Husband, Ex)
- The situation (Accidental, Forbidden, Secret)
- The twist (Revenge, Obsession, Hidden)
- The dynamic (My Enemy Husband, My Forbidden Bodyguard)

Examples:

- **Marrying My Enemy Billionaire** → Enemies to lovers, forced marriage
- **My Secret Mafia Husband** → Secret identity, forbidden romance
- **The Billionaire's Accidental Bride** → Accidental marriage, status gap
- **The Mafia King's Hidden Wife** → Hidden identity, possession, danger
- **When I Discovered My Husband Was My Enemy** → Reveal, betrayal, enemies-to-lovers

If your title conveys both **concept + trope**, you win.

ATTENTION-GRABBING TITLE FORMULAS THAT WORK

FORMULA 1: The Double Life

The Double Life of My (Status/Relationship)

- *The Double Life of My Billionaire Husband*
- *The Double Life of My Mafia Boss Fiancé*

Why it works:

- *Double life* promises secrets and betrayal
- Relationship word adds emotional stakes
- Status signals genre

FORMULA 2: The Secret Identity

My (Relationship's) Secret (Truth/Identity)

- *My Husband's Secret Identity*
- *My Bodyguard's Secret Mission*

Why it works:

- "Secret" is irresistible
- Signals mystery and danger
- Creates anticipation for the reveal

FORMULA 3: Status + Relationship

The (Adjective) (Status) (Relationship)

- *The Forbidden Mafia Prince's Revenge*
- *The Billionaire's Accidental Wife*

Why it works:

- It signals trope
- It signals genre
- It gives the entire concept in one line

FORMULA 4: The Verb Structure

(Verb)ing the (Status) (Relationship)

- *Marrying the Mafia Boss*
- *Seducing the CEO*

Why it works:

- Active
- Specific
- Implies clear stakes and tension

FORMULA 5: The Possession

(Status's) (Possession)

- *The Mafia King's Obsession*
- *The Billionaire's Revenge*

Why it works:

- Short
- Punchy
- High emotional voltage

FORMULA 6: The Reveal

When I Discovered (Shocking Truth)

- *When I Discovered My Husband Was the Mafia King*
- *When I Learned My Arranged Husband Was My Enemy*

Why it works:

- first-person intimacy
- huge twist
- pure clickbait

TITLE BUILDING BLOCKS

Mix and match:

STATUS WORDS:

- Billionaire
- CEO
- Mafia Boss
- Prince
- Alpha
- Doctor

RELATIONSHIP WORDS:

- Husband
- Wife
- Bride
- Fiancé
- Lover
- Boyfriend
- Ex

INTRIGUE WORDS:

- Secret
- Forbidden
- Double Hidden
- Dangerous

ACTION WORDS (examples):

- Marrying
- Betraying
- Escaping
- Seducing
- Discovering

TROPE WORDS:

- Accidental
- Arranged
- Enemy
- Forbidden
- Secret
- Hidden
- Revenge
- Fake (as in fake marriage)

THE TITLE CHECKLIST

Before you finalize, ask:

- Does it communicate my hook?
- Does it signal the *trope* instantly?
- Is the genre obvious?
- Would I click this?
- Does it feel addictive?
- Is it easy to remember and search?

If not, keep going.

WRITE MULTIPLE VERSIONS

Don't stop at one. Write ten variations. Pick the strongest.

Ask:

- Which one screams the trope the loudest?
- Which one communicates the conflict instantly?
- Which one would get the most clicks?

That's your title.

USING AI ETHICALLY FOR TITLE BRAINSTORMING

Use it only for:

- keyword lists
- variations
- brainstorming
- finding new combinations

You shape the final title. You are the creator.

THE TITLE IS PURE MARKETING

Your title is a promise.

A promise of:

- Conflict
- Desire
- Betrayal
- Danger
- Obsession
- Secrets
- Emotional chaos

If your title sells the trope and the hook, the viewer is already halfway in. Make it bold. Make it clear. Make it irresistible.

TAKE ACTION: STEP 7

1. Write 10 titles using the formulas above.
2. Make sure each version signals both: your **hook**, and your **trope**
3. Pick the strongest.

CHAPTER 8
LOGLINE & SYNOPSIS
MAKE PRODUCERS SIT UP

THE LOGLINE: YOUR SERIES IN ONE SENTENCE

YOUR LOGLINE MUST BE SO CLEAR AND SPECIFIC THAT A PRODUCER CAN picture the entire series instantly. No vague phrasing. No thematic descriptions. No generic "girl must learn to love again" language. A strong logline makes the reader think: **I know exactly what this series is, and I want to read Episodes 1–10.** Your logline must also match what actually happens in your script. Especially Episodes 1–10. If the promise and the execution don't match, the reader loses trust.

THE LONGER LOGLINE PARAGRAPH (55-70 WORDS)

Vertical series benefit from a longer, fuller logline, not the traditional 25–30 word feature-film version. Why? Because vertical dramas need to show their **story engine** upfront. This paragraph shows:

- Hook
- Escalating complication
- Direction of the series
- Emotional journey

- Stakes

Why this concept can sustain 40–70 episodes

Structure

Opening hook (1–2 sentences): The premise + inciting incident.

Complication (2–3 sentences): How the situation worsens, what increases the danger or emotion.

Stakes / direction (1–2 sentences): What's at risk and what the viewer will follow emotionally.

Total length: 55–70 words. One tight, visual, specific paragraph.

This is the version I personally recommend, the one I use in my own career, because it gives producers a full snapshot of the series without overwhelming them.

THE ONE-PAGE SYNOPSIS (250–300 WORDS)

Once your longer logline is clear, your next step is creating a **one-page synopsis**. This is not a beat sheet. Not an outline. Not a list of events. It's a single, polished page (250–300 words) that shows the entire **season arc** while still leaving room for discovery.

A strong one-pager communicates:

- Core relationship
- Main conflict
- The world
- Escalation pattern
- Emotional arc
- Midpoint shift
- Major complications
- General shape of the climax
- Tone and genre

Why this story is binge-worthy

You are not writing episode-by-episode details, you are giving a **macro view** of the emotional and narrative journey. Think of it as: Here's what the audience experiences from Episode 1 to Episode 40–70.

Structure of a strong one-pager:

Opening (3–5 sentences): Premise + inciting incident + setup of the main tension.

Escalation (8–12 sentences): How the danger, romance, or conflict deepens. Secrets. Betrayals. Reversals. The midpoint shift that changes everything.

Climax & resolution (4–6 sentences): Where the conflict explodes, how the emotional threads converge, and what kind of ending the audience can expect (happy ending, revenge victory, survival, new beginning, etc.).

Tone & promise (1–2 sentences): A final statement that reinforces the emotional journey and the addictive nature of the series.

This page proves the concept is solid and that YOU can sustain the arc.

COMMON SYNOPSIS MISTAKES

- Too much setup
- No escalation
- Listing events instead of showing consequences
- No emotional journey
- Too many characters
- Vague language
- Theme instead of story
- No sense of direction

Your job is clarity, escalation, and emotion, nothing else.

FORMATTING

Create one clean PDF:

Title_Logline_Synopsis_YourName

Include:

- Logline paragraph (55–70 words)
- One-page synopsis (250–300 words)
- Your name + email

Keep it simple and professional.

TAKE ACTION: STEP 8

Write:

1. Your 55–70 word long logline paragraph
2. Your 250–300 word one-page synopsis
3. Then ask yourself:
    - Does the logline hook immediately?
    - Does the synopsis escalate?
    - Does it show a real series engine?
    - Does it match Episodes 1–10?
    - Would YOU want to keep reading?

If yes, you're ready for the next chapter.

CHAPTER 9
CHARACTERS
SEND THEM SCREAMING INTO THE NEXT EPISODE

IIN THE FIRST TEN SECONDS, THE VIEWER MUST UNDERSTAND ALL THREE. From the moment a character appears on screen, the audience should know who this person is and why they matter in the scene.

- Who are they?
- What are they doing?
- What is your protagonist's goal?

Keep your villain simple but never one dimensional.

Your main character needs a clear, urgent goal that drives her through the entire series.

Example: Avenging her brother's death.

Vertical series thrive on **big character arcs**. Your protagonist can start weak, trapped, underestimated, or emotionally broken. The key is that she is in a position the audience does not want to be in.

We want viewers to empathize, not pity her. By the end of the series, she must evolve into someone powerful, capable, or transformed in a way the audience can see and feel.

Unlike a feature film, vertical dramas do not spend time on deep backstory. Character development is fast, clear, and driven by action.

CHARACTER BREAKDOWN

Your main characters need a simple and effective intro so viewers do not get lost. Producers may ask for character breakdowns alongside your logline, synopsis, and first ten episodes. A character breakdown includes:

- **First and last name, age, occupation**
- **Personality**
- **One paragraph** describing their crucial role in your story and their relationship to the other characters
- **Character Arc** (where they begin emotionally or situationally, and who they become by the end)

THE PROTAGONIST

- Do not make her pitiful.
- Do not make her passive.
- Do not make her a wimp (Unfortunately, sometimes they will ask you to do this at the start of the series).

Your audience needs to root for her from Episode 1. She should be someone cool, resilient, funny, clever, or brave. Someone viewers want in their girl squad.

In romance, the love interest must embody the fantasy. He, she, or they represent desire, hope, and yearning. Let the audience fall in love right along with your protagonist.

- Put two characters together in conflict or friction.
- Proximity plus tension creates chemistry.
- Make the dynamic loud and bold so the audience never wonders who likes who or who hates who.

By Episode 3:

- You must clearly establish the core relationship of your series.
- Make it obvious who the good guys are and who the bad guys are.
- Intrigue is not the same as confusion.

If your viewer ever asks "Wait… who is that again?" they will swipe to another series.

BUDGET CONSTRAINTS

Vertical dramas are low budget.

Aim for **six to ten characters maximum**.

Two leads, the rest supporting. Too many characters raise production costs and confuse your audience.

There is no time for backstory or slow introductions.

The viewer must understand who your main character is, what she is doing, and what is at stake right away.

CHARACTER DEVELOPMENT BALANCE

Avoid stereotypes, but also avoid overbuilding your characters.

You do not have the room for deep psychological excavation. On the other hand, do not underdevelop them. If viewers cannot emotionally connect, they will swipe away.

Your characters must be:

- Simple to understand
- Emotionally intense
- Instantly recognizable
- Driven by urgent motivations

Ask yourself:

- What is the worst thing that could happen to her?
- What is the most awkward situation she could land in?
- What is the most romantic?
- What is the most far-fetched or dramatic?

Do not be subtle. The vertical space is built on next level emotion. Be clear about what each character wants, and how their goals collide with others. Avoid similar sounding names.

The audience should never need to pause to remember who is who. In vertical series, characters are less about flaws and nuance, and more about urgency, secrets, lies, and pressure.

Everyone is hiding something, lying about something, or running from something.

START WITH ARCHETYPES THEN ADD HUMANITY

Here is the truth about vertical characters. Archetypes are not the enemy. In a 60 to 90 second episode format, you do not have time to slowly unveil personalities.

The audience must instantly recognize who someone is. Archetypes provide instant orientation. Traditional screenwriting teaches: Build complex, surprising, layered characters from the ground up.

Vertical writing teaches:

Start with recognizable types, then add depth through escalation, conflict, and action. You are not watering down complexity. You are delaying its reveal. You are making your story accessible, watchable, and addictive.

THE MOST RELIABLE VERTICAL ARCHETYPES

FEMALE LEAD ARCHETYPES

- **The Struggling Innocent:** Multiple jobs. A dependent family member. Pure-hearted but underestimated. Arc: Victim to Survivor to Victor.
- **The Secret Badass:** Appears ordinary but hides extraordinary skill. Arc: Hidden to Exposed to Unleashed.
- **The Ambitious Underdog:** Climbing her way out of a ruthless world. Arc: Nobody to Contender to Champion.
- **The Wealthy Heiress:** Privileged but emotionally empty. Arc: Privileged to Awakened to Purposeful.

MALE LEAD ARCHETYPES

- **The Ruthless CEO or Billionaire:** Cold exterior, wounded interior. Arc: Closed to Vulnerable to Redeemed.
- **The Scarred Mafia Heir:** Violent, loyal, emotionally guarded. Arc: Monster to Human to Protector.
- **The Fallen Prince:** Lost his power and identity. Arc: Broken to Rising to Restored.
- **The Secret Protector:** Watching from the shadows. Arc: Detached to Involved to Devoted.

SUPPORTING ARCHETYPES

- The Best Friend
- The Evil Ex
- The Disapproving Parent
- The Loyal Advisor
- The Rival
- The Innocent

These archetypes work because they are instantly readable, emotionally loaded, and culturally familiar.

You are not being lazy. You are being efficient.

TAKE ACTION: STEP 9

1. Create a cast of **six characters** for your concept.
2. For each character include:
   - **First and last name, age, occupation**
   - **Personality:** One paragraph describing their crucial role in your story and their relationship to the other characters
   - **Character Arc** (where they begin emotionally or situationally, and who they become by the end)

You now have the foundation of your cast.

CHAPTER 10
OUTLINING YOUR FIRST 10 EPISODES
START STRONG OR GO HOME

SPOILER WARNING: IF YOU HAVEN'T WATCHED *THE BLIND BRIDE of The Scarred Mafia Boss*, this chapter contains major plot reveals.

Note: *Blind Desire* was originally written as a **58-episode** vertical series.

TARGET FOR TODAY: EPISODES 1–10 OUTLINED

Ultimately, you will write a **tight outline for all 58 episodes**, with **one short paragraph per episode**.

This outline should be:

- Total 20 pages maximum
- Packed with visual details
- Clear enough that a producer can "see the series" instantly
- Aligned with what you agreed upon with the producer/director/platform rep

Before outlining, ask yourself:

- Where is my story headed?

- What escalating journey am I taking the audience on?
- How am I creating intimacy and urgency?

Intimacy + urgency = vertical success

WHAT EACH EPISODE OUTLINE MUST INCLUDE

For every single episode, keep it to **4–5 tight lines** and include:

- Where we are (location / situation)
- What happens (the on-screen action)
- Character reactions (emotional beats)
- What's revealed (new information)
- Cliffhanger clearly labeled

These five items create consistent vertical structure while keeping the reader hooked.

THE ENGINE OF EVERY EPISODE

Vertical storytelling runs on momentum. Your episodes are short, intense, and designed to be consumed fast. The viewer does not keep swiping because they love your world or your characters. They keep swiping because every episode delivers one clear thing:

Something changes.

Not later. Not eventually. In this episode. If nothing changes, the episode is filler. And filler kills retention. Every episode must deliver at least one of the following.

THE PLOT ADVANCES

Something concrete shifts the situation.

Examples:

- A secret is exposed

- A plan falls apart
- A character takes an action with consequences
- New information comes to light
- A lie gets revealed
- Someone is caught, discovered, or confronted

These are the gears of your story. If a gear does not turn, the machine stops.

THE STAKES RISE

The situation becomes worse, harder, or more emotional.

Examples:

- Pressure increases
- Someone loses power
- A relationship becomes more complicated
- A deadline or threat gets closer
- A new risk appears

Even a small rise in stakes counts, as long as it changes the viewer's emotional experience.

RELATIONSHIPS SHIFT

Vertical dramas thrive on micro shifts.

- One look can change everything.
- Trust improves or collapses
- Someone sees something they were not supposed to see
- A character lets down a guard
- A new bond forms
- Power dynamics tilt

A single glance can move the entire story forward.

THE SIMPLE RULE

Before you move on to the next episode, ask:

What changed? If the answer is "nothing," you do not have an episode. You have a placeholder.

Vertical storytelling rewards momentum. If you change something every time, the addiction builds. The viewer stays with you. The story pulls them forward one episode at a time. This is the engine that keeps them swiping up.

THE DOMINO EFFECT

A strong vertical series works like a line of dominoes.

- Episode 1 tips Episode 2.
- Episode 2 tips Episode 3.

Nothing resets. Nothing stands alone. Every episode creates the reason the next episode exists.

If an episode could be removed and nothing changes, it is a weak domino. You want each beat to cause the next beat.

Think in cause and effect, not "and then."

- She lies in Episode 3. So in Episode 4, that lie creates a problem.
- He hides evidence in Episode 5. So in Episode 6, someone almost finds it.
- They kiss in Episode 9. So in Episode 10, the fallout of that kiss explodes.

Every choice, secret, confession, or twist must push the story into the next complication.

THE DOMINO TEST

Look at your outline and ask for every episode:

- What changed in this episode
- How that change makes the next episode unavoidable
- What new problem, secret, or emotion is born right now

If you cannot answer those, you do not have a domino. You have a stall. Rewrite until each episode tips the next one forward.

CASE STUDY: THE BLIND BRIDE OF THE SCARRED MAFIA BOSS

To see how a complete vertical outline works in practice, study the Episode 1–10 breakdown below. These examples come directly from The Blind Bride of the Scarred Mafia Boss and show exactly how tight, visual, and hook-driven each episode should be.

EPISODE 1: "THE STANDOFF"

A tense meeting erupts between the Romano and Battisti crime families. Old grudges ignite. Guns are drawn. Insults blast across the table. Through the chaos, Eleanor Battisti sits perfectly still beside her father. Alexander Romano locks eyes with her. She never flinches.

Cliffhanger: Alexander wonders: *Is she blind?*

Why this works:

- 4–5 lines, sharp and visual
- Immediate conflict
- Introduces central characters in crisis
- Ends with a clean question cliffhanger

EPISODE 1 CHECKLIST

- Start at the inciting incident
- No setup, no routine
- 4–5 lines max
- Cinematic image
- Cliffhanger clearly labeled

EPISODES 2–9: RELENTLESS ESCALATION

Here's the escalation pattern from *The Blind Bride of The Scarred Mafia Boss*:

EPISODE 2: Eleanor agrees to marry Alexander to stop the war. Reveal: She's actually blind.

EPISODE 3: Eleanor's real mission: Find Matteo's medallion to prove Alexander killed her brother.

EPISODE 4: Alexander tests her blindness by throwing a knife at her face. She doesn't flinch.

EPISODE 5: Wedding day approaches, will either family show up?

EPISODE 6: Cold, political wedding. But the kiss? Undeniable chemistry.

EPISODE 7: At the Romano estate, Eleanor overhears Lorenzo call her a pawn.

EPISODE 8: Eleanor sees Alexander comforting a crying child, confusing everything she believed.

EPISODE 9: Eleanor sneaks into Alexander's study searching for evidence. Her father calls: Deliver results… fast.

Each episode **adds**, not repeats. Each beat **shifts the relationship**. Each cliffhanger **changes the dynamic**.

LAYERING COMPLICATIONS (WHILE...)

The engine of *Blind Bride* is its stacking complications:

Eleanor must hide her revenge mission

WHILE pretending to be blind

WHILE married to the man she believes killed her brother

WHILE falling in love

WHILE his family suspects her

WHILE her father pressures her for results

Each episode activates one or more of these layers.

This is vertical storytelling.

CHARACTER INTRODUCTION STRATEGY

Introduce your **entire core cast immediately**, ideally in **Episode 1** and often within **the first few seconds**. Vertical audiences do **not** have patience for slow reveals. They want to know **who the players are** right away, even if they don't yet know everyone's true agenda.

The Blind Bride example:

Episode 1: Alexander, Eleanor, Luca, Luca's daughters, Lorenzo, Marco, Luca's men

Episode 2: Deeper roles clarified (sister, ally, threat)

Episode 3+: Motivations expand, dynamics shift, but the cast is already known

Why this works:

- Gives viewers instant clarity
- Avoids confusion or "who is this now" fatigue
- Lets every character enter the story with purpose
- Allows you to build escalation instead of introductions

- Creates early emotional attachment to the ensemble
- Sets up relationships and conflict from episode one

By Episode 10, the viewer should:

- Know every key character
- Understand their base motivation
- Feel the tension between them

See how they fit inside the central relationship engine

THE CLIFFHANGER STRATEGY (EPISODES 1-10)

Your early cliffhangers must be powerful enough to capture free viewers who haven't paid yet.

Blind Bride cliffhangers:

- Question: Is she blind
- Revelation: She is blind
- Threat: If she finds proof, he dies
- Twist: She passes the knife test
- Choice: Will they show up to the wedding
- Emotional twist: Unexpected chemistry
- Threat: She's just a pawn
- Emotional shift: He's not the monster she thought
- Choice: Father demands loyalty
- Game-changer: She's not blind

Vary your cliffhanger types (see THE ART OF THE CLIFFHANGER for full breakdown):

- Questions
- Reveals
- Threats
- Emotional reversals
- Decisions

- Identity shifts

EPISODES 2–9: CHECKLIST

- Each episode escalates the previous one
- Complications layer, not repeat
- Vary your cliffhanger types
- Introduce characters through conflict
- Keep your protagonist active
- 4–5 lines per episode

EPISODE 10: THE PAYWALL HOOK

Episode 10 is the most important episode in the entire vertical model.

It must:

- Resolve a question
- Reveal something game-changing
- Raise the stakes
- Recontextualize Episodes 1–9
- Make paying feel inevitable

EPISODE 10: "UNVEILING"

Eleanor and Alexander share a rare moment of closeness. She gently asks about his scar. He refuses, embarrassed. Something shifts — they're finally connecting. He steps into the shower. Alone, Eleanor sits in the quiet, her face softening. She glances at the mirror. Then at him.

PAYWALL CLIFFHANGER: Eleanor can see. She is not blind.

Why this works:

- Resolves one emotional thread

- Reveals a massive truth
- Rewrites everything we've seen

Forces payment, viewers must know what her real plan is

EPISODE 10: CHECKLIST

- Resolves one major question
- Reveals a twist that raises stakes
- Forces the viewer to pay
- Re-contextualizes everything
- 4–5 lines only

TAKE ACTION: STEP 10

Write your outline for Episodes 1–10.

For each episode, include:

- Where we are
- What happens
- Character reactions
- What is revealed
- Cliffhanger clearly labeled
- 4-5 lines per episode.
- Make Episode 10 your biggest twist yet.

CHAPTER 11
FINISH THE OUTLINE

KEEP POURING GASOLINE ON THE FIRE

WARNING: If you have not watched *The Blind Bride of The Scarred Mafia Boss* (Working title: *Blind Desire*), spoiler alert. The following case study reveals major plot points from this series.

Note: *Blind Desire* was originally written as a 58-episode series. For this book, I recommend aiming for a **50-episode series** because it is easier to pace and structure. The principles in this chapter apply to any episode count between **40 and 70 episodes**.

EPISODES 11–20: POST-PAYWALL MOMENTUM

After the Episode 10 paywall reveal, you cannot let the momentum drop. Viewers just paid. Now you have to prove it was worth it.

CASE STUDY: *THE BLIND BRIDE OF THE SCARRED MAFIA BOSS*

Highlights from Episodes 11–20: These episode beats are simplified for teaching purposes, but notice how they keep the tension alive:

EPISODE 11: Eleanor asks Alexander to walk with her in the garden.

Their chemistry builds. She shares the (fake) story of losing her sight. They almost kiss. She pulls back, shaken.

EPISODE 12: A messenger arrives. There is a traitor in the Romano ranks. Eleanor panics, afraid they discovered her. But the accused is a Romano soldier. Alexander chooses banishment over execution. Everything she was told about his ruthlessness may be a lie.

EPISODE 13: Lorenzo tells Marco to watch Eleanor. Marco says she makes Alexander happy. Lorenzo answers, "He is not in love. He is blind."

EPISODE 14: Alexander invites Eleanor to a private dinner. No agenda, just time together. They share wine and laughter. Her guard drops. That night, Eleanor opens a drawer. She finds Matteo's medallion. And a note: "Next time, it is your life."

EPISODE 15: Alexander surprises Eleanor with a small carved wooden horse, a gift meant to comfort her. She softens. Later, she overhears soldiers preparing for a nighttime raid. She realizes the Romano family may strike sooner than she expected. Her mission just got more dangerous.

EPISODE 16: Eleanor makes tea for Alexander. Their dynamic is warmer, more intimate. He opens up about Matteo for the first time. His grief is real, raw. Eleanor's guilt spikes. That night, someone slips a letter under her door: "MOVE FASTER." The walls are closing in.

EPISODE 17: Lorenzo questions Eleanor directly. Too directly. He circles her with suspicion, testing every word she says. Eleanor barely holds the lie together. When he leaves, Marco warns her quietly: "Be careful. Lorenzo never asks a question he doesn't already know the answer to."

EPISODE 18: Eleanor returns to the Battisti home. Her father is cold, suspicious. "You are getting comfortable. Do not forget your mission." Alone, Eleanor whispers, "I do not know if I can finish what I started. "

EPISODE 19: Eleanor overhears a hushed conversation. An ambush is planned for Alexander in the morning. She manipulates him into staying home with her, saving his life. When he realizes what she did, they kiss for the first time.

EPISODE 20: Morning after their kiss. Luca Battisti arrives unannounced and meets Eleanor privately. She claims she is still loyal, that Alexander will die soon. Alexander stands in the doorway. He has heard something. Maybe not everything, but enough.

Why this works:

- Each episode moves the central question forward: Can Eleanor complete her mission, or has she fallen for her target
- New complications keep appearing: Traitors, threatening notes, family pressure, ambushes
- The relationship shifts from attraction to genuine emotional connection
- Episode 20 ends on a powerful cliffhanger that launches the next section

AVOIDING THE POST-PAYWALL SAG

The most common failure in vertical storytelling: Episodes 11–20 feel like filler. Nothing big happens. The story treads water. The audience drifts away. To avoid this, think in **action** → **consequence** → **complication**.

Bad pattern:

- **Episode 11:** They flirt
- **Episode 12:** They flirt
- **Episode 13:** They flirt
- **Episode 14:** They flirt
- **Episode 15:** They flirt

Good pattern:

- **Episode 11:** Action: She shares a vulnerable story.
- **Episode 12:** Consequence: He opens up in return.
- **Episode 13:** Complication: Someone notices they are getting too close.
- **Episode 14:** Action: She tries to pull away to regain control.
- **Episode 15:** Consequence: He pursues her emotionally anyway, which makes her conflict worse.

Also introduce **external pressure** here:

In *The Blind Bride of The Scarred Mafia Boss*, Episodes 11–20 combine:

- Internal conflict: Eleanor's growing feelings
- External threats: Lorenzo's suspicion, her father's orders, traitors, ambushes
- Relationship development: Chemistry turning into something real

The story does not plateau because **new layers of pressure** keep emerging. Build this section toward something specific. Episode 20 is not random. It is the setup for a major turn in the next block of episodes. Alexander overhearing Eleanor becomes fuel for future confrontation.

EPISODES 11-20 CHECKLIST

- Deliver on the promise of Episode 10
- Introduce new complications, not repetition
- Deepen emotional stakes between your leads
- Keep external pressure increasing
- No filler. Every episode must move the story forward
- Maintain 4–5 lines per episode in the outline

SUSTAINING MOMENTUM THROUGH EPISODE 50

You survived Episodes 1–10. Your paywall hook works. Episode 10 hits hard.

Now comes the hardest part: **Episodes 11–50**.

This is where most vertical series fall apart:

- The middle sags
- The story starts repeating itself
- The ending feels rushed

By the end of your outlining process, you want **Episodes 1–50** fully mapped:

- 10 episodes already outlined
- 40 more episodes to go
- Total outline length: around **25–30 pages**

This is a lot. So do not outline in strict order.

THE REVERSE-ENGINEERING METHOD

Do not outline Episodes 11–50 straight through from 11 to 50.

Instead:

1. Outline Episodes **1–10**

2. Jump to Episodes **41–50** and design your ending

3. Then return to Episodes **11–40** and build the bridge

Why this works

- You avoid a wandering middle. When you write forward with no clear destination, you often stall around Episodes 30–35 and start improvising.

- You know your destination. With Episodes 41–50 defined, the middle is no longer "what happens next" but "what must happen to earn this ending."
- The ending is not rushed. Since you design your last 10 episodes first, you are not scrambling at the end to tie everything together.
- You are not just asking, "What else happens?"
- You are asking, "What must happen to justify that final image?"

EPISODES 41–50: DESIGNING THE ENDING FIRST

Start with Episode 50.

Step 1: Write Your Final Image

- Forget plot for a moment. Focus on the **emotional resolution**.
- What is the final image of your series?
- What feeling do you want your audience to have as the last frame fades?

Examples:

- She walks down the aisle in a real wedding dress this time. He is waiting, emotional. This marriage is genuine, not political.
- He stands in sunlight for the first time in centuries. She is beside him, hand in hand. The curse is broken.
- She opens her bakery on a quiet morning. Months have passed. The bell rings. He walks in. One look is all they need.
- She deletes the revenge app and puts her phone away. No more obsession. She is finally free.

Write that as a **clear, visual Episode 50 beat**.

Step 2: Work Backwards – Episodes 45–49

Now ask yourself: "What has to happen in Episodes 45–49 to earn that final moment?"

Romance example:

Episode 50: Real wedding, honest love.

To earn that:

Episode 49: He makes a grand gesture that proves he has truly changed.

Episode 48: She must decide whether to forgive him or walk away.

Episode 47: He loses something major: Money, reputation, or family support.

Episode 46: She discovers the real reason he lied in the first place.

Episode 45: The final confrontation where every secret comes out.

Supernatural thriller example:

Episode 50: Curse broken, both alive, together.

To earn that:

Episode 49: The ritual succeeds.

Episode 48: She offers herself in a sacrifice that changes the rules.

Episode 47: They discover what the sacrifice actually requires.

Episode 46: The clan leader reveals the truth about the curse.

Episode 45: They are captured with no clear escape.

PLOT CLIMAX VS EMOTIONAL CLIMAX

Your audience cares about **how your characters feel** more than any single plot twist.

Plot climax: She wins the company back. Emotional climax: She tells her father she no longer needs his approval.

Plot climax: He defeats the rival. Emotional climax: She chooses him knowing the full truth.

Plot climax: The fake engagement contract ends. Emotional climax: He asks her to stay for real.

You need both. But if you have to choose, always protect the emotional climax.

Episodes 45–50 should deliver:

- The **big external resolution**
- The **deep emotional payoff**

EPISODES 49–50: LET THE ENDING BREATHE

Do not cram everything into Episode 50.

Episode 49: Immediate aftermath of the major confrontation. Healing, consequences, choices.

Episode 50: Epilogue. Show how life looks after everything that happened.

No new conflicts here. Only resolution, closure, and a sense of transformation.

EPISODES 35–40: THE MAJOR CRISIS

Once you have Episodes 41–50, work backward to your **crisis point**.

This is your "all is lost" stretch. Everything breaks so the ending can mean something.

Examples of crisis moments:

She is exposed as a spy. He finds out she has been lying about everything. He throws her out. She loses him, her mission, her cover.

The vampire clan captures him. He will be executed for choosing a human. She is powerless.

Her secret pregnancy is revealed in front of everyone at the worst possible moment. She is humiliated. He says nothing.

The fake engagement is exposed to the press. Both their reputations crash. They blame each other.

Episodes 35–40 are about:

- Things falling apart
- Hitting rock bottom
- Choosing whether to give up or fight

A possible pattern:

Episode 35: The truth explodes.

Episode 36: Public or private fallout.

Episode 37: Despair. They pull away.

Episode 38: A tough conversation with a mentor, friend, or even antagonist.

Episode 39: Clarity about what they really want.

Episode 40: The decision to fight for that desire, no matter the cost.

Now episodes 41–50 are about executing that choice.

BUILDING THE BRIDGE: EPISODES 11-40

At this point you know:

- Where Episode 10 leaves off
- Where your crisis hits (Episodes 35–40)
- Where and how the story ends (Episodes 41–50)

Now you build the bridge.

EPISODES 11-25: DEEPENING COMPLICATIONS

You are planting the seeds of your crisis.

Ask:

What needs to be true for that Episode 35 crisis to feel inevitable?

If the crisis is "fake engagement gets exposed":

Episodes 11–25 might include:

- Someone growing suspicious
- Lies piling up and becoming harder to maintain
- Photos, documents, or recordings that could expose them
- A journalist or rival sniffing around
- The couple getting more comfortable and careless

If the crisis is "he discovers she has been lying about everything":

Episodes 11–25 might include:

- Small lies that turn into bigger ones
- Moments where she almost tells the truth
- Him noticing inconsistencies but wanting to believe her
- Her dragging other people into the lie
- The emotional stakes rising as she falls for him

You are not adding random drama. You are **setting up the destruction**.

THE MIDPOINT TURN (EPISODES 23-27)

Around Episode 25, something major should shift.

Before the midpoint: Things happen to your protagonist. They react.

After the midpoint: Your protagonist makes a clear choice. They act.

Examples:

- She has been hiding the pregnancy. In Episode 25, she decides to tell him herself. She walks into his office ready to confess, only to be blindsided by a new twist.
- He has been hiding that he is a vampire. In Episode 25, he reveals himself to save her.
- She has been in the fake relationship only for money. In Episode 25, she realizes she is in love with him. The stakes are suddenly real.
- Avoid a midpoint sag where the same thing happens again and again.

Bad version:

Episode 11: She almost gets caught

Episode 15: She almost gets caught

Episode 19: She almost gets caught

Good version:

Episode 11: She almost gets caught

Episode 15: She tells a bigger lie to cover the first lie

Episode 19: The bigger lie creates a new threat

Episode 23: She is forced to involve someone else who now has leverage

Each complication creates a new problem.

EPISODES 26–34: BUILDING TO THE CRISIS

You are now slowly tightening the spring toward the Episodes 35–40 crisis.

If the crisis is exposure:

- The antagonist gathers proof
- The protagonist leaves a trail without meaning to

- The couple grows closer, making the betrayal hurt more
- The trap is set
- If the crisis is a brutal breakup or rejection:
- Trust deepens
- Vulnerability grows
- Keeping the secret becomes harder
- The cost of telling the truth rises

By Episode 34, it should feel like you are standing on the edge of a cliff.

SECONDARY CHARACTERS AND SUBPLOTS

You cannot sustain 50 episodes on the main couple alone.

Episodes 18–30 are a great place to give secondary characters moments to shine:

- Best friend's subplot
- A secondary romance
- Villain's backstory
- Shifts in family dynamics

These arcs should still intersect with your main story. They keep the world rich and give emotional texture without stealing focus.

THE SUSTAINABILITY QUESTION

As you outline Episodes 11–40, keep asking:

Can my concept truly sustain 50 episodes

Red flags:

- The same conflict repeats without escalation
- Cliffhangers feel recycled
- You keep introducing new characters just to create "stuff"
- Your protagonist becomes passive

If that happens, consider:

- Adding new **layers of complication** that grow from your core conflict
- Simplifying and returning to your central engine
- Or accepting that this concept might be better suited for a feature, not a 50-episode vertical series

It is better to pivot early than to force a weak series into existence.

TAKE ACTION: STEP 11

Complete your **full outline for 50 episodes**.

Use this order:

Episodes 1–10: Already done in the last chapter

Episodes 41–50: Design your ending first

Episodes 35–40: Design your major crisis

Episodes 11–34: Build the bridge between paywall, midpoint, crisis, and resolution

For each episode, write:

- Where we are
- What happens
- Character reactions
- What is revealed
- Cliffhanger (clearly labeled)

Keep each episode to **4–5 lines**. Total outline length: **25–30 pages**.

When you finish this, you will have something most writers never manage:

A complete, professional vertical series blueprint.

CHAPTER 12
THE POLISH PASS

SHINE IT UNTIL
THEY SAY YES

MOST WRITERS THINK: "OUTLINE DONE. TIME TO SCRIPT." THIS IS THE fastest way to lose weeks of work. This chapter exists to polish and secure approval before writing a single line of script. If you draft 50 episodes from an unapproved outline and the producer says "change the ending," "cut a character," or "the middle drags," you have just burned days you cannot get back. Polishing now prevents disaster later.

WHAT YOU HAVE AFTER OUTLINING

You should now have:

- 25 to 30 pages
- Episodes 1 to 50 outlined (4 to 5 lines per episode)
- Every episode with a labeled cliffhanger
- Character arcs mapped

It is solid. But it is not submission ready.

ONE MORE THING

This is what you do before sending anything to a producer.

- **Logic**: Fix holes. Restore cause to effect. Make sure every development has a reason.
- **Cliffhangers**: Strengthen them. Vary the types. Avoid repetition.
- **Arcs**: Clarify the emotional journeys. Make sure transformations track.
- **Pacing**: Remove sags. Prevent a rushed ending. Combine weak episodes.
- **Budget**: Consolidate locations. Reduce night scenes. Simplify action.
- **Paywall**: Make Episode 10 irresistible. This is your conversion moment.

When this pass is complete, the outline is ready for approval.

OPTIONAL BUT POWERFUL: AI FEEDBACK

AI cannot replace your taste or your producer's expectations, but it can serve as fresh eyes for pattern detection. Paste this prompt with your outline:

Prompt:

I have completed a 50 episode vertical outline (60 to 90 seconds per episode). Each episode is 4 to 5 lines with a labeled cliffhanger.

Please analyze and provide:

- 5 to 10 weakest episodes, with reasons
- Cliffhanger variety and any repetitive types
- Pacing issues (Episodes 21 to 40 sagging? 40 to 50 rushed?)
- Character arc gaps
- Logic holes

- Stakes escalation assessment
- Strength of Episode 10 paywall cliffhanger, with fixes
- Budget red flags (locations, night scenes, complex action)
- Repetitive patterns
- Overall strengths to protect
- Be specific with episode numbers and actionable fixes.

How to use it:

- Read fully.
- Fix the major issues first: Weak episodes, logic holes, Episode 10, arc gaps.
- Then adjust pacing, repetition, and budget.
- Only after that do fine-tuning.

THE CLIFFHANGER DOUBLE CHECK

Run this audit across Episodes 1 to 50:

- Every episode has a labeled cliffhanger
- Types are balanced
- Episodes 1 to 30 are your strongest (free to paywall retention)
- Episode 10 is the strongest hook of all
- No two consecutive episodes use the same type

Examples of stronger alternatives:

- Revelation: She finds a photo. Matteo and Alexander together. Friends?
- Threat: Lorenzo steps forward. "We talk. Now."
- Choice: A text from her father: "Two weeks. Finish it or I will."
- Twist: Alexander whispers, "Eleanor… I know you are not blind."

End your series with revelation, threat, choice, or twist. Make the audience feel something.

STORY LOGIC, ARCS, AND PACING

Motivation: Are turns earned? If someone betrays, forgives, or falls in love, you must justify why it happens now. Add seeds or pressure.

Cause to Effect: Every beat needs a visible link: Discovery to decision to consequence. Plant breadcrumbs for reveals.

Pacing: Sagging middle (Episodes 20 to 30): Combine weak episodes. Add deadlines, rivals, or exposure risk.

Cramped ending (Episodes 40 to 50): Allow room for payoff. Escalate, breathe, then strike.

STAKES ESCALATION

Episodes 1 to 10: If caught, she loses the mission

Episodes 11 to 20: If caught, she loses him

Episodes 21 to 30: If caught, both families kill them

Episodes 31 to 40: If caught, war erupts

Episodes 41 to 50: If caught, she loses herself and her identity

If stakes plateau, add external pressure or raise consequences.

PREEMPTIVE BUDGET ADJUSTMENTS

1. Location consolidation

- Aim for 5 to 7 primaries.
- Merge duplicates.

Examples:

- Ep14 restaurant → Estate dining room
- Ep28 restaurant two → Secondary compound office
- Ep48 banquet hall → Existing estate hall redressed

2. Night ratio

Keep night episodes at or below 30 percent unless genre demands it. Convert to dusk, early morning, or interior options.

3. Cast count

- Main (40+ episodes): 3 to 5
- Recurring (10 to 30 episodes): 3 to 5
- Supporting (1 to 10 episodes): 5 to 10
- Merge small parts into recurring roles.

4. Action complexity

- High budget scenes can be replaced with:
- Aftermaths
- Reversals
- Clues
- Intimate confrontations with prop stakes

THE POLISH PASS: THE WORDS THEMSELVES

Clarity: Who does what, why it matters, and what changes.

Visual writing: Use actions and gestures, not abstractions.

Brevity: Stay within 4 to 5 lines per episode. Cut padding.

Episode titles: Use intriguing hints. Avoid bland labels.

Formatting:

- Title page.
- Logline.
- Synopsis (250 to 300 words).

- Characters.
- Numbered and titled episodes.
- Labeled cliffhangers.
- Page numbers.

Line trim example

- Before: "She walks slowly into the study, nervously looking around."
- After: "She slips into the study, checks the hall, rifles the desk."

SUBMITTING FOR APPROVAL

When the polish is done, submit the outline.

Subject: [Series Title] Complete Outline for Approval [Your Name]

Email body:

Hi [Producer Name],

Attached is the complete 50 episode outline for [Series Title]. I strengthened cliffhangers (Episode 10 optimized for paywall), consolidated locations, and escalated the stakes through the full arc. Please share notes whenever ready. I will wait for approval before scripting.

Best,

[Your Name]

THE 48 HOUR WAIT

Do not script during this time.

Use the wait to:

- Rest your brain
- Prepare script templates

- Organize your calendar
- Work on other projects

Golden rule: No scripting until approval.

WHAT HAPPENS NEXT

Most common: Notes. Fix them in 2 to 4 hours. Resubmit. Wait.

Sometimes: Instant approval. Begin scripting.

Rare: Major changes. Hop on a call, realign, revise. Still cheaper than rewriting 50 episodes after the fact. This polish pass saves 20 to 40 hours of rewriting and makes you look professional.

THE POLISH PASS CHECKLIST

- Every episode has a labeled cliffhanger
- Cliffhanger mix balanced; Episode 10 strongest
- Logic clean; motivations earned
- No pacing sags; ending spacious
- Stakes escalate by tier
- Locations consolidated; cast count disciplined
- Night scenes controlled; action simplified
- Weak episodes strengthened or combined
- Writing clear, visual, concise
- Professional formatting
- Outline submitted for approval
- No scripting until approval

TAKE ACTION: STEP 12

1. Polish your 50 episode outline.
2. Run the cliffhanger audit.
3. Fix weak episodes.
4. Strengthen Episode 10.

5. Streamline locations.
6. Clarify arcs.
7. Prepare your outline for approval and wait for notes.

When the outline is approved, you are ready for THE ART OF THE CLIFFHANGER.

CHAPTER 13

THE ART OF THE CLIFFHANGER
MAKE THEM SMASH THAT NEXT EPISODE BUTTON

Vertical series live and die by one thing: the hook. Not most episodes. Not some. All of them. If you do not hook your viewer in the final three to five seconds, they swipe away and the series is over for them. A cliffhanger is not decoration. It is the engine that drives the swipe. No hook equals no swipe. No swipe equals no series.

HERE'S THE PSYCHOLOGY BEHIND IT

Vertical viewers are not sitting down for a scheduled experience. They are on their phones, often multitasking, often distracted, and always ready to abandon you. The thumb is the most impatient tool in entertainment. If the viewer senses a slow beat, a gentle fade out, or a scene that resolves before the cut, they swipe away without hesitation.

You have three seconds to keep them. Three seconds to trigger curiosity, urgency, emotion, or danger. Your job is to keep them swiping up, not swiping away.

The examples in this chapter come from *The Blind Bride of the Scarred Mafia Boss*, the vertical series I wrote and that many of you have watched. These are not invented moments. They are real hooks that held real audiences and helped turn the show into a number one series, trending for more than six weeks as of December 2025.

This is the most important chapter of the book. If you master this, you can write vertical series that grip viewers from Episode 1 all the way to Episode 60.

THE NON NEGOTIABLE RULE

Every episode ends with a hook. Every single one. The entire episode is a staircase that leads to the last five seconds. Not the middle. Not the beginning. The end. Tape this rule to your wall. Treat it like law.

THE CLIFFHANGER CHECKLIST

Before you lock an ending, it must pass all eight tests:

- Does the final beat create urgency right now?
- Is the hook specific, not vague.
- Did I reveal something before cutting?
- Did I cut before the natural resolution?
- Can the viewer predict the next shot within three seconds.
- Did I pay off or complicate the previous hook immediately?
- Is this hook different from the last two or three?
- Will the payoff feel equal to or bigger than the setup.
- If you fail even one, rewrite the ending.

WHAT MAKES A CLIFFHANGER WORK

A cliffhanger must create urgent emotional or psychological need. Not mild interest. Not a soft tease. Not gentle anticipation. The viewer should feel a pull in their body to swipe up. They need to know what happens in the next beat.

- **Bad cliffhanger:** "I wonder what she will do tomorrow."

- **Good cliffhanger:** "I need to know what happens in the next five seconds."

Vertical storytelling is immediate, specific, and high stakes.

THE DUN, DUN, DUN TEST

Read your ending out loud. Then add "DUN, DUN, DUN."

If it lands, the hook works.If it sounds silly, the hook is weak.

"You are not blind." DUN, DUN, DUN. Works.

"We should talk tomorrow." DUN, DUN, DUN. Falls flat.

This test is a great way to see if what you're doing is working.

THE TEN TYPES OF VERTICAL CLIFFHANGERS

Every strong hook falls into one of these ten categories.

Rotate them to avoid repetition and keep your audience swiping.

TYPE 1: THE REVEAL

A reveal drops information that changes the story right now.

Weak: "I have something to tell you."

Strong: *The Blind Bride* – **Episode 21:** An assassin attacks their bedroom. Eleanor fights him off with trained precision. Alexander watches her. Her movements are too fast. Too accurate. Too intentional. The assassin escapes. Alexander turns to her.

> ALEXANDER: You are not blind.

One line collapses twenty episodes of deception.

Use reveals wisely. They only work when the truth is big.

TYPE 2: THE REVERSAL

A reversal flips the dynamic within seconds. Safety becomes danger. Love becomes threat.

Weak: "Everything will be fine."

Strong: *The Blind Bride* – **Episode 40**: Eleanor and Alexander are finally intimate. Clothes come off. Walls fall away. They are connected and vulnerable. Lorenzo bursts in, bleeding, warning that Luca has ordered a hit on Eleanor. Alexander protects her and throws Lorenzo out. The door closes. Eleanor stands still. Her hand slowly moves behind her back. She pulls a hidden knife to his face (I was thrilled when I thought of that).

> ELEANOR: It is the only way my father will take me back. You have to die, Alexander.

Instant reversal. Complete shift.

TYPE 3: THE QUESTION

Not a casual question. A question that demands the next episode for the answer.

Weak: "What should we do next?"

Strong: *The Blind Bride* - **Episode 15**: Alexander finally confesses he did not kill Matteo. Someone else set them up. He failed Matteo, and he has lived with that guilt. Eleanor listens.

> ELEANOR: If you did not kill Matteo, then who did?

A question that forces the swipe.

TYPE 4: THE THREAT

Danger arrives or is promised with immediate impact.

Weak: "You will regret this."

Strong: *The Blind Bride* - **Episode 27:** Eleanor drinks wine with her father. Luca watches her carefully.

> LUCA: I heard you and Alexander are in love.
> A good reason to celebrate.

She hesitates. Her vision begins to blur. Her knees buckle.

> LUCA: As I suspected, you have already
> betrayed me.

She collapses. A threat that becomes real in seconds.

TYPE 5: THE INCOMPLETE SCENE

You cut right in the middle of an action or confession.

Weak: "We need to talk."

Strong: Eleanor decides she cannot go through with the wedding. She leaves her room. At the same moment, Alexander turns the corner. They collide.

> ALEXANDER: Are you having doubts?
>
> ELEANOR: Indeed. And you?
>
> ALEXANDER: Nerves.

They stand close. Breath held. CUT.

No resolution. Maximum pull.

TYPE 6: THE EMOTIONAL SHIFT

A character changes internally in a way that alters the story.

Weak: She watches him leave. CUT. No shift.

Strong: Eleanor sits alone in the garden. A little girl cries nearby after falling from her bicycle. Alexander kneels, cleans her knee, and comforts her calmly.

> ALEXANDER: My father used to say scars
> are proof that we healed.

The girl smiles and runs off. Eleanor touches her mother's locket.

> ELEANOR (VO): You are not who I thought
> you were.

The relationship changes, and the viewer wants to see what she does next.

TYPE 7: THE OFFER

A proposal that could change everything if accepted or refused.

Weak: "We should work together someday."

Strong: He slides the contract across the table.

> HIM: One signature. One million dollars. One
> condition — you never speak to your sister
> again.

She stares at the pen. Her hand trembles.

A strong offer freezes the viewer in the space between yes and no. The tension is in the decision   not the answer.

TYPE 8: THE POWER SHIFT

Control changes hands instantly. One character gains leverage, dominance, or advantage, and the other loses it. This shift is *felt*, not just stated. The scene flips not because of new information, but because someone now holds emotional, physical, or moral power.

Weak: "I think I might break up with you one day."

Strong: *The Blind Bride – Episode 40:*

Eleanor and Alexander finally let their walls down. Breathless. Vulnerable. Soft. The first moment they both want the same thing.

Lorenzo interrupts, wounded, warning that Luca ordered Eleanor's death. Alexander protects her, shuts Lorenzo out. Silence. Close. Intimate again.

> ELEANOR: You have to die, Alexander.

They were lovers *one second ago*. Now she holds the power.

Viewers swipe because they need to know who survives the shift. Use this type when a character takes control, betrays, flips a dynamic, or exposes leverage. A *Power Shift* must change the balance of the story immediately.

TYPE 9: THE OBJECT CLUE

A physical item appears, disappears, or changes hands, revealing something important without dialogue. It plants suspicion, exposes secrets, or connects emotional dots for the audience. The hook is visual and immediate.

Weak: She finds a note that says, "We need to talk tomorrow."

Strong: *The Blind Bride – Episode 12:*

Eleanor returns to her room. Everything looks normal. She reaches for her pillow. Beneath it sits Matteo's medallion. The medallion that should be buried with him. Her breath stops. A message carved on the back. "TRAITOR."

No conversation. No explanation. One object shifts the entire story.

A clue works because it forces the viewer to search for meaning. They need the next episode to understand who put it there, when, and why. It turns a simple prop into fuel.

Use Object Clues to escalate mystery, deepen character suspicion, or ignite new plot lines. Keep them clear and loaded with consequence. Not generic items. Evidence.

TYPE 10: THE INTERRUPT

Tension builds. A moment peaks. Just as the scene is about to resolve or explode, something slams into it and stops everything. No answer. No outcome. No release. The story is forced to continue.

Weak: "They were about to kiss, but she got nervous."

(Small feeling. No disruption. No cliff.)

Strong: *The Blind Bride – Episode 46:* Eleanor and Alexander are in bed. Breathless. Consumed. The most intimate they have ever been. BANG. The door bursts open.

> SERENA (O.S.): Get your hands off her.

Serena stands in the doorway, sword drawn.

The audience swipes because something urgent just crashed into the moment. No explanation. No aftermath. No choice but to continue.

Interrupts work best when they hit at the peak of tension — sexual, emotional, or violent — and rip the scene open before it can land.

STRATEGIC CUTTING

Traditional storytelling resolves a beat. Vertical storytelling cuts one beat before it resolves.

To show you exactly what this means, let us take a sequence from *The Blind Bride*.

In a traditional film or TV script, the following would appear inside one continuous scene:

- Eleanor finds Matteo's medallion.
- She confronts Alexander.
- He confesses the truth.
- She decides whether she can trust him.

One scene. One emotional arc.

Vertical storytelling turns that one scene into several episodes. You are not adding material. You are splitting the emotional beats into separate hooks.

Here is the vertical version:

Episode 14: Eleanor finds Matteo's medallion on her pillow with a death threat.

Episode 15: Alexander tells her the truth about Matteo. Eleanor asks, "If you did not kill him, then who did?"

Episode 16: Alexander confronts Lorenzo. Lorenzo says, "She must be taken out."

Episode 17: Eleanor overhears Luca planning an ambush on Alexander. Same story. Four episodes instead of one scene. Four hooks instead of one emotional resolution.

You find the resolution point, then you cut one beat before it.

REMEMBER

Not every scene needs a hook. Every episode does.

Inside an episode, you can breathe. You can let your characters feel and think. But the ending must snap the story forward.

You are not writing scenes that end naturally. You are writing momentum that never stops.

This is the art of the cliffhanger.

TAKE ACTION: STEP 13

1. Label the type of cliffhanger for each episode.
2. Run every ending through the checklist.
3. Do the DUN, DUN, DUN test.
4. Strengthen or replace any weak hooks.

5. Avoid repeating the same type several times in a row.

Master this chapter and you will master the vertical series format.

You will know how to keep viewers swiping up and staying with you far beyond Episode 1.

CHAPTER 14
THE BLIND BRIDE — CLIFFHANGER ANALYSIS

HOW I KEPT THE AUDIENCE HOOKED

EPISODE 1 – THE STANDOFF

Cliffhanger Type: Question

SETUP: TWO MAFIA FAMILIES FACE OFF ACROSS A WAREHOUSE. FINGERS near triggers. Tension thick enough to slice. One wrong word could start a war. Eleanor sits perfectly still in the chaos. Calm. Unshaken. Alexander watches her. Trying to understand her.

Cliffhanger:

> ALEXANDER: So that's the blind girl
> everyone's been talking about?

Why it works: The conflict is immediate. No setup required. The ending plants one obsessive question in the viewer's mind. Curiosity becomes the hook that pushes them into Episode 2.

What writers can learn: A first episode should end with a direct question that demands the next episode for the answer. If the viewer does not feel compelled to swipe immediately, the hook needs to be stronger.

EPISODE 2 — THE TREATY

Cliffhanger Type: Threat

Setup: Alexander proposes marriage to end the war. Luca offers Eleanor. In a side room, Luca reveals Eleanor is his weapon — sent to destroy Alexander from inside. Eleanor accepts the marriage without hesitation. Everyone is stunned. Later, Lorenzo warns Alexander.

Cliffhanger:

> ALEXANDER: You think she's here to kill me?
>
> LORENZO: If she is... let's hope she misses.

Why it works: The bride is now a potential assassin. The audience knows she has a mission. Alexander suspects but doesn't know. This gap between what the viewer knows and what the character knows creates tension that demands resolution.

What writers can learn: Early episodes should establish threat. Give your audience a reason to fear for your protagonist — even if the danger wears a wedding dress.

EPISODE 3 — SUSPICIONS

Cliffhanger Type: Reveal

Setup: Eleanor tells Serena her true mission — find Matteo's medallion and kill Alexander if the rumors are true. Alexander visits Eleanor. She touches his face, his scars, reads him by hand. Flirtation mixed with danger. Then he tests her. Slashes a knife near her face. She doesn't flinch.

Cliffhanger:

> ALEXANDER (V.O.): She is blind after all.

> ALEXANDER: I'll see you on our wedding
> day.

Why it works: Alexander believes he has confirmed she's blind. The audience knows she passed a test — but doesn't yet know if she's faking. Suspicion sharpens. The hook isn't an answer. It's a false confirmation that makes us doubt even more.

What writers can learn: A reveal doesn't have to expose truth. It can deepen mystery by showing a character reach the wrong conclusion.

EPISODE 4 – FIRST IMPRESSIONS

Cliffhanger Type: Emotional Shift

Setup: Wedding day. Alexander prepares, tense. Lorenzo warns him this is suicide. Alexander tells him to watch Eleanor — and not hesitate if something happens.

In the guest room, Serena fastens their mother's locket around Eleanor's neck. Eleanor hesitates.

Cliffhanger:

> ELEANOR: You're right. This is crazy. I can't
> do this.

She grabs her cane. Walks to the door.

Why it works: Doubt. After three episodes of mission and masks, Eleanor cracks. Will she run? Will she go through with it? The emotional shift — from soldier to vulnerable woman — makes us need to see what she does next.

What writers can learn: An emotional shift cliffhanger works when a character's internal state changes in a way that could alter everything. Doubt is powerful. Use it.

EPISODE 5 — THE WEDDING

Cliffhanger Type: Incomplete Scene

Setup: Eleanor steps out of her room. Alexander turns the corner at the same moment. They collide. An unplanned encounter. Both nervous. Both hiding something.

Cliffhanger:

> ALEXANDER: Are you having doubts?
>
> ELEANOR: Indeed. And you? Nerves setting in?
>
> ALEXANDER: I'm afraid so.

They stand close. Breath held.

Why it works: The scene is unfinished. Two enemies about to marry, both admitting fear, standing inches apart. No resolution. No kiss. No retreat. The brain hates incomplete business — and that's exactly why it works.

What writers can learn: You don't need an explosion to create urgency. Sometimes standing still — breath held, words hanging — is enough.

EPISODE 6 — VOWS AND VENDETTAS

Cliffhanger Type: Threat

Setup: The wedding. Tension on both sides. Hands near weapons during the vows. They exchange rings. Kiss briefly. Walk the aisle.

At the reception, Luca dances with Eleanor and whispers a reminder: she knows what she has to do. Alexander cuts in.

Cliffhanger:

> ALEXANDER: What did your father say
> to you?
>
> ELEANOR: Reminded me that I'm a Battisti.
>
> ALEXANDER: Not anymore.

Why it works: Eleanor's loyalty is the question. She's now in Alexander's house, wearing his ring, carrying her father's mission. The threat is invisible but everywhere. "Not anymore" is a claim — not a certainty.

What writers can learn: A threat cliffhanger doesn't need a gun. Sometimes a single line of dialogue carries more danger than a weapon.

EPISODE 7 – NEW TERRITORY

Cliffhanger Type: Incomplete Scene

Setup: Alexander shows Eleanor her new room. He's made accommodations for her blindness — nothing moves without warning. A small kindness.

He's called away. Eleanor explores alone. Later, she descends the staircase. Graceful. Composed. Then she stumbles. Her cane slips. She falls forward.

Alexander catches her. One arm around her waist. Bodies close.

Cliffhanger:

> ALEXANDER: I've got you.

Why it works: Physical contact. Breath held. The scene stops at the height of tension. No resolution. No next line. Just two bodies pressed together and silence.

What writers can learn: Incomplete scenes work best when you cut at the moment of maximum tension — not after it resolves. Let the audience imagine what comes next.

EPISODE 8 — BENEATH THE SURFACE

Cliffhanger Type: Emotional Shift

Setup: The staircase moment continues. Eleanor thanks him. He hands back her cane with a joke. She walks away, composure restored. Alexander tells Lorenzo his wife stays. End of discussion.

Later, Eleanor sits in the garden. A young girl cries nearby — scraped knee from a bicycle fall. Alexander kneels beside her. Comforts her. Shows his scar. Tells her scars mean we healed. Eleanor hears everything.

Cliffhanger:

> ELEANOR (V.O.): You're not who I thought
> you were, Alex Romano.

Why it works: Her perception shifts. The man she was sent to kill just showed tenderness to a child. The enemy becomes human. This emotional turn changes everything — and the audience knows it before she does.

What writers can learn: The most powerful cliffhangers aren't always external. An internal shift — a change in how one character sees another — can be just as gripping.

EPISODE 9 — SHADOWS AND SECRETS

Cliffhanger Type: Question

Setup: Eleanor searches Alexander's study. Opens a drawer. Fingers skim a sealed folder. Footsteps. Lorenzo enters. She plays innocent — claims she's lost. He directs her to her room. She leaves, tapping her cane. Lorenzo checks the drawer. It's slightly open. He doesn't trust her. Later, Lorenzo reports to Alexander. She was in your study. The drawer was open. Alexander stays by the window. Reflecting.

Cliffhanger:

> ALEXANDER (V.O.): Maybe Lorenzo's right.
> Maybe I've let my guard down. She is a
> Battisti, after all… But then why do I want to
> believe her?

Why it works: Internal conflict. Alexander is caught between suspicion and desire. The question isn't answered — it's asked. And the audience asks it with him.

What writers can learn: A question cliffhanger can be internal. When your protagonist doubts themselves, the audience doubts with them. That uncertainty is the hook.

EPISODE 10 – TOUCH

Cliffhanger Type: Reveal

Setup: Alexander confronts Eleanor. You were in my study. She denies. Tension rises. He grabs her wrist. She slaps. He catches her hand. They freeze. Inches apart. Then she steps forward. Rips his shirt open. Touches the scar on his chest. Reads him like braille.

The tension turns electric. He almost kisses her. Pulls away. Goes to shower. Eleanor crosses to the mirror. Watches herself. Then turns slightly — catches a glimpse of him in the doorway. Towel. Nothing else. She looks. A small smile.

Cliffhanger:

> ELEANOR (V.O.): Not bad. Alexander
> Romano, how will you react when you realize
> I'm not blind.

Why it works: The audience learns the truth. She can see. She's been faking. Everything we thought we knew shifts. This isn't a reveal to a character — it's a reveal to us. And now we're complicit in her secret.

What writers can learn: A reveal cliffhanger is most powerful when it changes the rules of the story. Now the audience knows something the protagonist doesn't. That gap creates unbearable tension.

EPISODE 11: TENSION

Cliffhanger Type: Threat / Question

Alexander receives a warning letter.

> ALEXANDER: Someone in the house… is a traitor.
>
> ELEANOR: Who is it?
>
> ALEXANDER: It doesn't say.
>
> ELEANOR (V.O.): Are they talking about me?

Danger introduced. Identity unknown.

EPISODE 12: THE TRAITOR

Cliffhanger Type: Emotional Shift

Alexander shows mercy to a traitor. Eleanor watches.

> ELEANOR (V.O.): They said he was ruthless. That he'd kill without hesitation. But he did none of that. Everything everyone has told me about Alexander Romano was a lie.

Her view of him transforms again.

EPISODE 13: THE LIEUTENANT

Cliffhanger Type: Incomplete Scene

Dinner ends. Alexander reveals Matteo was his friend. Eleanor doesn't believe him.

>ELEANOR: Thank you for dinner.
>Enlightening, in its own way.

She walks out.

>ALEXANDER (V.O.): What were you thinking?
>Why would she believe you?

Confession rejected. Tension unresolved.

EPISODE 14: THE TRUTH BETWEEN US

Cliffhanger Type: Offer / Question

Eleanor confronts Alexander with Matteo's medallion. He swears innocence.

>ALEXANDER: Can you trust me?

Eleanor stares at him... But doesn't respond.

The question hangs. No answer given.

EPISODE 15: CONFESSIONS

Cliffhanger Type: Question

Alexander confesses everything about the night Matteo died.

>ELEANOR: If you didn't kill Matteo... then
>who did?

The central mystery sharpens.

EPISODE 16: THE MEDALLION

Cliffhanger Type: Power Shift

Lorenzo leaves Alexander's study, dismissed.

> LORENZO (V.O.): She's clouded his judgment. She must be taken out.

Lorenzo decides to act. He becomes the threat.

EPISODE 17: SUMMONS

Cliffhanger Type: Threat

Eleanor overhears Luca planning an ambush on Alexander.

> LUCA (O.S.): He leaves at dawn. That's when it happens... Clean. Quick. Just make sure Eleanor isn't in the car.

Eleanor stiffens. Backs away.

Immediate danger. She has information.

EPISODE 18: SUMMONS (PART 2)

Cliffhanger Type: Question

The convoy is hit. Alexander survived because Eleanor asked him to stay.

> ALEXANDER: You knew, didn't you? You saved me?

Accusation or gratitude? The answer matters.

EPISODE 19: RECKONING

Cliffhanger Type: Incomplete Scene

Alexander and Eleanor finally give in. Passion. Heat.

ALEXANDER: Do you want to disappear?

ELEANOR: Sometimes.

They lie in silence.

Intimacy achieved. But what comes next?

EPISODE 20: TREASON

Cliffhanger Type: Threat

Luca confronts Eleanor. Gives her one week.

LUCA: One week.

He kisses her cheek. Exits.

Deadline set. The clock starts.

EPISODE 21: INSTINCT

Cliffhanger Type: Reveal

An assassin attacks. Eleanor fights him off with trained precision. Alexander watches.

ALEXANDER: You're not blind.

Twenty episodes of deception collapse in one line.

EPISODE 22: AFTERMATH

Cliffhanger Type: Emotional Shift

Eleanor confesses everything. Alexander listens.

>ELEANOR: The man I can't lie to anymore.

>ALEXANDER: Then don't.

They kiss. Truth. Love.

Trust rebuilt through honesty.

EPISODE 23: THE KNIFE INSIDE

Cliffhanger Type: Emotional Shift

Eleanor insists Lorenzo is the traitor. Alexander resists.

>ALEXANDER: I hate that you might be right.

His loyalty cracks.

EPISODE 24: THE POISONED WELL

Cliffhanger Type: Incomplete Scene

Lorenzo confronts Alexander. Accusations fly.

>LORENZO: Twenty years. Like brothers you
>and I. And you pick her over me.

Alexander doesn't respond. Lorenzo walks out, upset.

Brotherhood fractured. No resolution.

EPISODE 25: THE BETRAYAL

Cliffhanger Type: Power Shift

Lorenzo meets Luca in secret. Offers to trade Eleanor for a debt.

LUCA: You'd trade her... for a debt?

Lorenzo hesitates... then nods.

Alliances shift. Lorenzo crosses the line.

EPISODE 26: THE RETURN

Cliffhanger Type: Threat

Alexander confronts Lorenzo. Eleanor enters.

ELEANOR: Then they'd better be ready.
Because we'll take them all down.

Battle lines drawn.

EPISODE 27: DANCING WITH THE DEVIL

Cliffhanger Type: Threat

Eleanor drinks wine with Luca.

LUCA: As I suspected, you've already
betrayed me.

Her vision blurs. Her knees buckle. She collapses.

Poisoned. Captured. Immediate danger.

EPISODE 28: DOUBLE AGENT

Cliffhanger Type: Offer

Eleanor begs Serena for help. Asks her to turn against their father.

> SERENA: One chance, sister. Don't squander it.

She drops the key at Eleanor's feet.

Serena chooses. The offer accepted.

EPISODE 29: THE BREAKING POINT

Cliffhanger Type: Incomplete Scene

Eleanor escapes. Serena meets her in the alley.

> SERENA: That didn't take long.

> ELEANOR: I've had practice.

They disappear into the dark — together.

Escape in progress. Destination unknown.

EPISODE 30: THREADS IN THE DARK

Cliffhanger Type: Emotional Shift

Alexander learns Eleanor was captured.

> ALEXANDER: I'll kill every last one of them if that's what it takes to bring her home.

Love declared through rage.

EPISODE 31: DANGEROUS GAMES

Cliffhanger Type: Incomplete Scene

Alexander prepares to rescue Eleanor. Lorenzo appears.

> LORENZO: You sure you want to do this?

> ALEXANDER: I am.

> LORENZO: Well then… good luck.

Alexander slips into the alley.

Mission begins. Outcome unknown.

EPISODE 32: RUN

Cliffhanger Type: Emotional Shift / Object Clue

Serena is shot. Eleanor gives her their mother's locket.

> SERENA: You get to live. Don't make it for nothing.

Eleanor runs. One last glance back.

Sacrifice. Loss. The locket passes hands.

EPISODE 33: THE MESSAGE

Cliffhanger Type: Reveal

Luca admits to Lorenzo that he killed Matteo.

> LUCA: It never stopped me before.

> LORENZO: Matteo… that was you?

> LUCA: You're welcome.

The truth exposed. Luca is the killer.

EPISODE 34: ASHES

Cliffhanger Type: Emotional Shift

Alexander finds Eleanor's bloody shirt and the locket. Guards confirm she's dead.

ALEXANDER: Eleanor...

He breaks.

Grief. Devastation. False death.

EPISODE 35: REUNION

Cliffhanger Type: Interrupt

Alexander mourns in the garden. Eleanor appears alive.

They kiss. Then — attackers emerge from the shadows.

Reunion interrupted by violence.

EPISODE 36: CROSSROADS

Cliffhanger Type: Power Shift

Alexander declares Eleanor is family. Lorenzo walks out.

Lines drawn. Lorenzo leaves.

EPISODE 37: THE DIVIDE

Cliffhanger Type: Offer

Marco urges Alexander to strike. Alexander hesitates.

> ALEXANDER: The next move starts a war.

> ELEANOR: Do it.

She decides. War begins.

EPISODE 38: THE NIGHT IT ALL BEGAN

Cliffhanger Type: Reveal

Alexander's nightmare reveals a memory — Luca was at the warehouse when Matteo died.

> ALEXANDER: It's your father. He was there.

Eleanor's expression shifts. Stunned to cold.

The final piece of the puzzle.

EPISODE 39: WAR COUNCIL

Cliffhanger Type: Incomplete Scene

Eleanor presents strategy. Lorenzo says he trusts her — but she has to leave. Alexander and Eleanor turn to each other.

Decision pending. What will they choose?

EPISODE 40: THE SAFE HOUSE

Cliffhanger Type: Reversal

Eleanor and Alexander are intimate. Vulnerable. Lorenzo interrupts with news of a hit on Eleanor. Alexander throws him out. The door closes. Eleanor reaches behind her back. Pulls a knife.

> ELEANOR: It's the only way my father will
> take me back. You have to die.

Lover becomes killer. Total reversal.

EPISODE 41: THE QUEEN RETURNS

Cliffhanger Type: Reveal

Eleanor returns to Luca. Claims she killed Alexander. Presents the medallion.

> LUCA: Welcome home, my daughter.

He embraces her.

Is she playing him? The audience knows more than Luca.

EPISODE 42: THE PRODIGAL DAUGHTER

Cliffhanger Type: Reveal

Eleanor mourns Serena. Then —

> SERENA (O.S.): What about me?

Serena stands in the doorway. Alive.

> ELEANOR: Serena? I thought you were—

Death reversed. Serena lives.

EPISODE 43: SISTERS AND SPIES

Cliffhanger Type: Incomplete Scene

Serena confirms she's alive. They embrace.

Reunion. But what comes next?

EPISODE 44: THE LINE

Cliffhanger Type: Reveal

Eleanor vomits. Touches her stomach.

> ELEANOR: Oh... A child?

Pregnancy revealed.

EPISODE 45: SISTERS IN SHADOWS

Cliffhanger Type: Reveal / Interrupt

Serena leaves. Eleanor hears a noise. Spins with knife drawn.

It's Alexander. Bruised. Breathing hard.

> ELEANOR: You're supposed to be dead.

He's alive. Inside enemy territory.

EPISODE 46: THE BLADE AND THE BODY

Cliffhanger Type: Interrupt

Eleanor and Alexander are in bed. Passion. Need.

BANG. Door slams open.

SERENA (O.S.): Get your hands off her.

Serena stands in the doorway — sword drawn.

Caught. Confrontation forced.

EPISODE 47: NO SAFE HAVEN

CLIFFHANGER TYPE: QUESTION

Eleanor confronts Serena. Tells her the truth about Luca.

ELEANOR: Do you stand with us… or against us?

Serena must choose. Answer withheld.

EPISODE 48: THE CLAIM

Cliffhanger Type: Power Shift

Eleanor overhears Luca's plan.

LUCA (O.S.): She signs in a week — and every Romano captain's replaced... The Romano dynasty ends.

ELEANOR (V.O.): My own father setting traps... But if he thinks I'll be his weapon again... He's forgotten who forged me.

She has information. Power shifts to her.

EPISODE 49: POWER VACUUM

Cliffhanger Type: Threat

Lorenzo and Marco unite against Eleanor.

LORENZO: We reclaim what's ours—

MARCO: —or bury her beside him.

Alliance formed. Eleanor targeted.

EPISODE 50: THE FIRST STRIKE

Cliffhanger Type: Threat

Eleanor prepares the dinner. Picks up a knife.

SERENA: They won't come unarmed.

ELEANOR: Neither will I.

Battle approaches.

EPISODE 51: THE SETUP

Cliffhanger Type: Incomplete Scene

Everyone prepares for the dinner. Lorenzo and Marco arrive.

LORENZO: This smells like a setup.

MARCO: Good. I was getting bored.

Eleanor in her black dress.

SERENA: You look like a queen.

ELEANOR: More like bait.

The trap is set. Dinner begins.

EPISODE 52: THE PEACE DINNER – PART I

Cliffhanger Type: Reveal

Eleanor announces she carries the heir to both bloodlines. Then — the doors open. Alexander enters. Alive.

LORENZO: They said you were dead.

Double reveal. Pregnancy and resurrection.

EPISODE 53: THE PEACE DINNER – PART II

Cliffhanger Type: Question

Luca exposes Lorenzo's betrayal.

ALEXANDER: Lorenzo, did you...?

Lorenzo doesn't answer.

Accusation lands. Guilt uncertain.

EPISODE 54: REDEMPTION

Cliffhanger Type: Reversal

Eleanor orders the guards to seize Luca.

ELEANOR: Seize my father. For conspiring in the murder of my brother.

The guards pause — then close in.

Daughter arrests father. Power flips.

EPISODE 55: RECKONING

Cliffhanger Type: Emotional Shift

Serena asks Luca to deny it. He stays silent.

> ELEANOR: Justice delayed… is justice served. Tonight — we end the cycle.

Luca is chained.

> ALEXANDER: The old world dies tonight.

Justice served. Era ends.

EPISODE 56: BROTHERHOOD

Cliffhanger Type: Threat / Incomplete Scene

Luca grabs a dagger. Lunges at Alexander. Lorenzo throws himself in front. The blade sinks into Lorenzo's side.

> ALEXANDER: Stay with me.

Sacrifice. Life uncertain.

EPISODE 57: LEGACY

Cliffhanger Type: Emotional Shift

Lorenzo pledges himself to the house. To peace.

> ALEXANDER: You're my brother. Always.

Redemption complete.

EPISODE 58: RECONCILIATION

Cliffhanger Type: Offer

Alexander proposes they leave. Let Serena lead.

> ELEANOR: And if she says yes?
>
> ALEXANDER: Then we walk.
>
> ALEXANDER (V.O.): Let the age of kings die in our wake.

A new path offered.

EPISODE 59: NEW ORDER

Cliffhanger Type: Emotional Shift

Serena and Lorenzo accept leadership together.

> ALEXANDER: Battisti-Romano. United at last.
>
> ELEANOR: No more war rooms. Only peace.

Resolution. Unity achieved.

EPISODE 60: FULL CIRCLE

Cliffhanger Type: Resolution

Eleanor and Alexander in the garden. She names the baby Mattea.

> ELEANOR: No crowns. No war. Just us.

They kiss. End. *No cliffhanger. The story closes.*

TAKE ACTION: STEP 14

Sharpen your cliffhangers so every episode ends on a hook.

1. Rewrite the final beat of each episode to cut **one moment before resolution.**
2. Strengthen urgency. Raise a question, drop a reveal, imply danger, or shift emotion.
3. Remove soft endings. No goodbyes, no fade-outs, no tidy wrapping.
4. Swap passive endings for active ones. Something must **change or threaten** to change.
5. Try two alternate endings for each weak hook. Pick the one that punches harder.
6. Vary cliffhanger types so momentum stays fresh.
7. Read your ending out loud. If you do not feel the pull to continue, rewrite.

Your job is not to end the scene. Your job is to make the viewer swipe.

When this step is done, every episode should snap forward and demand the next one.

CHAPTER 15
DIALOGUE AND VOICE-OVERS
MAKE THEM KISS, FIGHT, OR DIE TRYING

MAKE EVERY WORD COUNT

Vertical series dialogue is different from traditional screenwriting. Every word must earn its place. You do not have time for naturalistic rambling, long speeches, or clever banter that does not move the story. In vertical, dialogue should do at least two of these three things at the same time:

- Reveal character
- Advance plot
- Set up or pay off a cliffhanger

If a line does not do at least two of those, cut it.

THE GOLDEN RULE: 2 TO 3 SENTENCES MAXIMUM

In traditional screenwriting, characters can talk in paragraphs. In vertical, they cannot.

Maximum dialogue block: 2 to 3 sentences

Ideal dialogue block: 1 to 2 sentences

Why:

- Screen time is short: 60 to 90 seconds per episode
- Viewers are on phones: Long blocks are hard to read
- Pacing is fast: Slow dialogue kills momentum
- Attention span is limited: if it drags, they swipe away
- Think sharp, not verbose.

BEFORE AND AFTER EXAMPLES

Example 1: The Confession

Before (traditional):

> SARAH: I need to tell you something, and I
> don't know how you're going to react. I've
> been thinking about this for weeks,
> rehearsing what I would say, but now that
> we're here, I realize there's no easy way to
> do this. The truth is, I've been lying to you.
> Not about everything, but about something
> important. The night your brother died? I was
> there. I saw what happened.

After (vertical):

> SARAH: I need to tell you something. The
> night your brother died? I was there.

What we cut:

- Setup ("I've been thinking about this")
- Self-awareness ("I don't know how to say this")
- Buildup that stalls the moment

What we kept:

- The essential information
- The emotional impact

- A strong cliffhanger setup

Example 2: The Threat

Before (traditional):

> MARCUS: You think you're so smart, don't you? Walking in here like you own the place. Let me tell you something about how things work in this family. When someone disrespects me the way you just did, there are consequences. Serious consequences. You might want to reconsider your approach before someone gets hurt. And I'm not talking about me.

After (vertical):

> MARCUS: You just made a mistake. When someone disrespects me, there are consequences. (beat) And I am not talking about me.

What we cut:

- Rhetorical questions
- Explaining what we are about to show
- Redundant phrases
- What we kept:
- The threat
- The implication that someone else will get hurt
- The tension

Example 3: The Revelation

Before (traditional):

ELENA: I don't even know where to begin. This whole situation is so complicated. You think you know who I am, but you don't. Not really. I've been hiding something from you since the day we met. Something that changes everything between us. My father - the man you've been trying to destroy - he's not just my father. He's your father too.

After (vertical):

ELENA: You think you know who I am. You don't. My father? He is yours too.

What we cut:

- "I don't know where to begin"
- "This is complicated"
- All the preamble
- What we kept:
- The misdirect
- The gut punch reveal
- The implications

DIALOGUE TECHNIQUES FOR VERTICAL

1. Cut Greetings and Goodbyes

You do not need hellos.

Do not write:

INT. COFFEE SHOP - DAY

Sarah enters. Spots Mike.

SARAH: Hey.

MIKE: Hey. Thanks for coming.

SARAH: Of course. How are you?

MIKE: Good. You?

SARAH: Fine. So, listen -

Write:

INT. COFFEE SHOP - DAY

Sarah sits across from Mike.

SARAH: We need to talk about last night.

Start scenes late. Get to the point immediately.

2. Interrupt Before Completion

Characters do not need to finish every thought.

ALEX: The reason I called is because I –

JORDAN: Do not. I already know.

Interruptions feel real, build tension, and keep pace tight.

3. Use Silence

Sometimes the strongest line is no line at all.

INT. BEDROOM - NIGHT

Emma holds up a positive pregnancy test. David stares. His face goes white.

No dialogue. The moment speaks for itself.

4. Subtext Over Text

Characters should rarely say exactly what they mean.

Do not write:

> ANNA: I am still in love with you and I am
> scared you do not feel the same way.

Write:

> ANNA: Do you ever think about us?

The subtext is clear. She still loves him, and she is terrified he does not feel the same. It becomes more interesting because she is not saying it directly. She is circling the truth instead of announcing it.

5. Conflict In Every Exchange

Even simple lines should carry tension.

Boring:

> LISA: Want coffee?
>
> TOM: Sure. Thanks.

Better:

> LISA: Want coffee?
>
> TOM: Since when do you care what I want?

Even in small talk, find an angle.

VOICE-OVER IN VERTICAL SERIES

Voice-over is powerful in vertical. Used well, it can:

- Reveal internal thoughts
- Speed up exposition
- Create intimacy with the protagonist
- Maintain pace while conveying information

When To Use VO

Use VO when:

- You need to convey emotional state fast
- Spoken dialogue would bog the scene down
- You want contrast between what they say and what they think
- You need to establish world or rules quickly
- Avoid VO when:
- You can show it visually
- Regular dialogue can handle it
- It simply repeats what is already on screen

VO Rules For Vertical

Rule 1: Keep it brief

One sentence. Two maximum.

Rule 2: Let VO contrast with action

What they think versus what they do is tension.

Example:

INT. WEDDING - DAY

Elena walks down the aisle toward Alexander.

        ELENA (VO): I am here to destroy him.

She smiles, takes his hand.

Action and VO are in conflict. That is the hook.

Rule 3: Use VO for internal decisions

Example:

INT. OFFICE - NIGHT

Sarah stares at a USB drive full of her boss's secrets.

> SARAH (VO): I could end him right now.

She deletes the files. Drops the drive in the trash.

> SARAH (VO): Or I could end myself.

VO shows the internal war. Action shows the choice.

Rule 4: Use VO to sharpen cliffhangers

Example:

INT. CAR - NIGHT

Marcus drives. Unknown number flashes on his phone. She knows.

Marcus freezes.

> MARCUS (VO): How is that possible I
> covered everything.

Cliffhanger: Someone knows his secret. The VO amplifies his fear.

COMMON DIALOGUE MISTAKES

Mistake 1: Exposition Dumps

Do not write:

ANNA: As you know, your father and I have been married for twenty years, and ever since he started his company fifteen years ago, things have been difficult between us, especially after your sister moved to California three years ago, which is why I think we need to talk about what happened last Thursday when I found out about -

Do this:

ANNA: I know about Thursday.

Get to the point. Let visuals and context do the rest.

Mistake 2: On The Nose Dialogue

Do not write:

MARK: I am angry at you because you betrayed me.

Write:

MARK: Get out.

His action and tone communicate everything.

Mistake 3: Overwriting

Do not write:

LISA: I just think that maybe, if we are being honest with each other, which I hope we are, that perhaps we should consider the possibility that this might not be working the way we thought it would.

Write:

> LISA: This is not working.

Simple. Clear. Strong.

Mistake 4: Identical Character Voices

Every character should sound distinct.

Test: cover the names. Can you still tell who is speaking?

If not, separate their voices by:

- Vocabulary (formal vs casual, slang vs precise
- Sentence length (short bursts vs full sentences)
- Rhythm (fast, clipped, or slow and thoughtful)
- Attitude (cynical, optimistic, sarcastic, blunt)

DIALOGUE POLISH CHECKLIST

After writing your script, run this checklist:

- Every dialogue block is 3 sentences or less
- No greetings or goodbyes unless they reveal character
- Exposition is kept off the dialogue whenever it can be shown
- Every line does at least two of: Reveal character, advance plot, set up cliffhanger
- Subtext is stronger than text
- There is some tension in every exchange
- Each character has a distinct voice
- No one repeats the same idea twice
- VO is brief and adds contrast, not repetition
- You have read it out loud and it sounds spoken, not written

THE DIALOGUE RHYTHM TEST

- Read your scene out loud.
- Does it sound like real people under pressure?

- Does it sound like a writer performing on the page?

If it feels written, simplify.

Tips for natural rhythm:

- Use contractions (do not becomes don't)
- Use sentence fragments
- Let characters cut each other off
- Let emotion break grammar
- Let people repeat a word or phrase when upset

EXAMPLE: POLISHING A SCENE

First draft:

INT. LIVING ROOM - NIGHT

Emma enters. Sees David packing a suitcase.

>EMMA: What are you doing?
>
>DAVID: I am leaving. I cannot stay here anymore.
>
>EMMA: You cannot just leave. We need to talk about this.
>
>DAVID: There is nothing to talk about. I made my decision.
>
>EMMA: But what about us What about everything we have been through?
>
>DAVID: I am sorry, Emma. I just cannot do this anymore.

He closes the suitcase. Walks to the door.

>EMMA: Please do not go.
>
>DAVID: Goodbye, Emma.

He leaves. Emma cries.

Polished draft:

INT. LIVING ROOM - NIGHT

Emma enters. Stops. David packs a suitcase. EMMA: You are leaving.

> DAVID: Yeah.
>
> EMMA: Because of her.

He stays silent. Zips the suitcase.

> EMMA: Say something.
>
> DAVID: What do you want me to say?
>
> EMMA: That you love me. That this was a mistake.

He picks up the suitcase. Heads for the door.

> EMMA: David -
>
> DAVID: I am sorry.

He leaves. The door clicks shut.

Emma stares at the door. Her phone buzzes.

> ON SCREEN: "He is mine now."

Cliffhanger: The other woman is watching.

What improved:

- Less dialogue, more impact
- Subtext instead of explanation
- Clear emotional power balance
- A visual, modern cliffhanger (the text message)

DIALOGUE AND VOICE-OVERS: FINAL THOUGHT

In vertical series, dialogue is a scalpel, not a paintbrush.

Every word must be intentional. Every line must do real work.

If a line does not move the plot forward, reveal character, or set up a cliffhanger, it does not belong in your script.

Your mantra: Shorter, sharper, faster.

TAKE ACTION: STEP 15

1. Highlight every dialogue block longer than three sentences. Cut it down.
2. Remove greetings and goodbyes that do not reveal character.
3. Replace exposition lines with visual or behavioral choices where possible.
4. Add subtext. Make characters imply rather than explain.
5. Read your scenes out loud. If anything sounds written instead of spoken, simplify.
6. Check that each character has a unique voice.
7. Confirm that every line does at least two of these three:
   - Reveals character
   - Advances plot
   - Sets up or pays off a cliffhanger

Once you have leaned out and sharpened your dialogue, you are ready for the next step.

CHAPTER 16
WRITING THE FIRST 10 EPISODES

SHOCK THEM, SEDUCE THEM, PULL THEM IN

THE MOST IMPORTANT EPISODES OF YOUR SERIES

- Episodes 1 to 10 are the most important part of your vertical series:
- Episode 1 hooks your audience.
- Episodes 2 to 9 retain your audience.
- Episode 10 converts viewers beyond the paywall.

If Episodes 1 to 10 do not work, nothing else matters.

You do not earn the right to write a beautiful Episode 37 if viewers never make it past Episode 3. This chapter is about turning your outline into tight, shootable scripts for Episodes 1 to 10.

Before we jump into the craft, let's get the technical stuff out of the way so you know exactly how to format and structure your scripts.

SOFTWARE TO USE

Use any professional screenwriting software that exports standard screenplay format. The most common choices are:

Final Draft - WriterDuet - Highland - Fade In - Celtx

All of these handle industry-standard formatting automatically. What matters is that your scripts look professional and consistent.

FORMATTING

Vertical series scripts follow the exact same formatting rules as traditional TV or film scripts. Same margins. Same scene headers. Same dialogue blocks. Same action lines.

The difference is length and tightness. Episodes are one to two pages, so your action lines must be lean. Every line needs purpose. Write visually. Keep the read fast.

To structure your script clearly:

EPISODE 1: Title of the episode (I like to give my episodes titles)

SCENE 1-1 (Episode 1, Scene 1)

SCENE 1-2 (Episode 1, Scene 2)

Then:

EPISODE 2: Title of the episode

SCENE 2-1

SCENE 2-2

This numbering system keeps the script organized for producers, editors, and translators, especially when scenes are pulled apart or reordered during production.

If you want to see what this looks like on the page, download BONUS #3 the 10 first episodes of *The Blind Bride of the Scarred Mafia Boss*: http://21dayscreenplay.com/bookbonuses

Use it as your visual reference for pacing, layout, and how tight the writing must be.

DIALOGUE REMINDERS

Verticals are dialogue driven. Do not strand the audience in silence with no emotional anchor.

Keep these rules in front of you while you write:

- Maximum 2 to 3 sentences per character turn.
- Break long thoughts into separate beats and lines.
- Cut greetings and goodbyes unless they reveal character.
- Every line of dialogue must do at least one of these, and ideally two:
- Advance the plot
- Escalate conflict
- Reveal character under pressure

If a line does not do any of these, cut it.

FLASHBACKS: USE ONLY AS BOMBS

Flashbacks are not seasoning. They are bombs.

Use a flashback only when it:

- Lands emotionally in a big way
- Acts as visual proof of something important
- Moves the story forward in the present

Ask yourself:

- Does this flashback change how we understand the present?
- Does it answer a crucial question or deepen a mystery?
- Is there a simpler way to convey this through behavior right now?

If the answer is no, you do not need the flashback.

EPISODE 1: START WITH THE INCITING INCIDENT

Episode 1 opens on conflict and image. No long setup. No ordinary world. No warm up. Drop the audience directly into the moment everything changes.

Examples:

- The breakup
- The proposal
- The arrest
- The car crash
- The wedding that is actually a deal

Your job in Episode 1:

- Show your protagonist in action
- Make the stakes clear
- Hint at the core relationship or central conflict
- End on a strong, specific cliffhanger
- By the end of Episode 1, the audience should know:
- Who the main character is
- What kind of world this is
- What is at stake
- What kind of show they are getting

EPISODES 2 TO 9: BUILD AND ESCALATE

Episodes 2 to 9 are your retention engine.

This is where most series lose viewers or make them addicted.

Across Episodes 2 to 9, you should:

- Layer complications, one on top of another
- Deepen the central relationship or core conflict
- Reveal secrets in stages
- Introduce only the characters you truly need

Every episode still follows the same vertical basics:

- One clear situation
- One strong emotional turn
- One sharp cliffhanger

Ask yourself as you go:

- Did this episode change something?
- Is the situation different at the end than at the beginning?
- Did I repeat a beat from a previous episode, or did I escalate it?

If an episode feels like a repeat, adjust the problem so it creates a new complication, not the same one again.

EPISODE 10: THE PAYWALL HOOK

Episode 10 is the most important cliffhanger in your entire series.

This is your paywall moment.

The hook that makes viewers decide to pay, subscribe, or keep watching. Episode 10 should:

- Resolve one of the big questions from Episodes 1 to 9
- Reveal a new piece of information that changes everything
- Raise the stakes in a way that feels impossible to ignore

Popular Episode 10 moves:

- The big lie is exposed
- The protagonist is not who they claimed to be
- The relationship crosses a line it cannot uncross
- The villain makes a move that feels irreversible
- A secret pregnancy, betrayal, identity, or deal comes to light

If Episode 10 does not feel like a punch to the gut or a door opening into an even bigger story, keep rewriting until it does.

WRITING CHECKLIST FOR EPISODES 1 TO 10

As you script Episodes 1 to 10, use this checklist:

- Every episode is labeled and ends on a strong, clear, varied cliffhanger
- Dialogue: Maximum 2 to 3 sentences per character turn, no monologues
- Descriptions and action lines are minimal and visual, not literary
- Episode 1 starts with the inciting incident, opens on conflict and image
- Episode 10 delivers your strongest hook, the paywall moment
- Each episode is 1. 5 to 2 pages maximum
- Cliffhanger types vary from episode to episode
- Visual storytelling is clear enough for viewers who watch without sound
- Budget is respected: 3 to 6 locations total, small cast, minimal night scenes

If an episode fails more than one of these checks, tighten it before moving on.

TAKE ACTION: STEP 16

1. Write full scripts for Episodes 1 to 10.
2. Label every episode and end each one on a strong, specific cliffhanger.
3. Keep dialogue blocks short, 2 to 3 sentences per turn, no monologues.
4. Strip descriptions down to what the camera can see and what matters emotionally.

5. Make sure Episode 1 opens on the inciting incident.
6. Make sure Episode 10 delivers your strongest hook and paywall twist.

Once you have ten tight, high impact episodes, you are ready to carry that momentum through the rest of the series.

CHAPTER 17
COMPLETING YOUR FIRST DRAFT
FINISH THE DAMN THING

You've completed Episodes 1 to 10. Now we move into the middle and late episodes of your series. For simplicity in this book, we'll use **"50 episodes" as a reference point**, but your series may be longer or shorter. Everything in this chapter applies whether you're writing 40, 50, 60, or more episodes. Think of "Episode 50" as **"your final episode,"** not a fixed number.

AS YOU WRITE TOWARD THE END OF YOUR SERIES:

- **Apply cliffhanger principles:** Use the five types, keep them varied, and run each one through the DUN DUN DUN test.
- **Build to your major crisis:** Around the three-quarter mark (for example, Episodes 35–40 in a 50-episode series), everything should break.
- **Do not rush the ending:** Your final stretch (Episodes 41–50, if using 50 as reference) needs breathing room to land emotional and narrative payoffs.
- **Track your page count:** Adjust as needed based on your actual episode count.
- **Complete your full draft:** "Episode 50" = shorthand for reaching the end.

STRUCTURAL REMINDERS FOR THE MIDDLE TO FINAL EPISODES

Below is the standard structure for a 50-episode series. If your series has more or fewer episodes, adjust proportionally.

Episodes 11 to 20: Post-Paywall Momentum

After Episode 10, viewers are committed. Deliver immediately.

- Follow through on the Episode 10 hook
- Introduce new complications and reversals
- Deepen relationships and emotional stakes
- Build toward the midpoint (around Episode 25)

Episodes 21 to 30: Deepening Complications

This section escalates everything.

Mid-series pivot around Episode 25

- Raise stakes in every episode
- Multiple threats begin intersecting
- Plant seeds for the crisis that will erupt later

This is your second act pressure cooker.

Episodes 31 to 40: The Crisis Build

This is where everything collapses.

- Every situation gets worse
- Lies unravel
- Secrets emerge
- Relationships fracture

The "all is lost" moment hits between Episodes 35–40. If you're writing more than 50 episodes, this crisis shifts later, but the structure stays the same.

Episodes 41 to 50: The Final Movement (or "'Til the End")

Here, "Episode 50" is simply the *reference ending*.

This is the space where you resolve arcs, confront the core conflict, and deliver your emotional payoff.

- Protagonist takes decisive action
- The final confrontation happens
- Emotional climax outweighs plot mechanics
- You close threads and fulfill promises

The final episode ends with a transformed version of your opening image

If your series is 60+ episodes, this "final movement" begins later. Use this section to think in *ratios*, not exact numbers.

PACING REMINDERS

No matter your series length, never cram your resolution into the last few episodes.

Your final episodes (41–50 in our reference structure, or the final 20 percent of your total) need enough space to:

- Resolve conflicts
- Pay off emotional promises
- Show true transformation
- Deliver a powerful final image

Rushing your ending makes even the strongest series fall flat.

PAGE COUNT TRACKING

Use this formula no matter how many episodes you're writing:

(Total page cap – Pages written so far) ÷ Episodes remaining = Target pages per episode

Check your page count after each episode past the first 10. Adjust as needed.

FIRST DRAFT CELEBRATION

When you finish your final episode, whether that's Episode 50 or Episode 78, celebrate it. You wrote an entire vertical series. Most writers never finish. You did. But don't send it yet. The next chapter is your polish and tightening pass.

WHAT TO DO NOW

- Save multiple copies
- Back up in the cloud
- Step away for at least a day
- Clear your mind for your polish pass. Fresh eyes will transform your draft

TAKE ACTION: STEP 17

1. Finish writing through to *your final episode*.
2. Apply consistent cliffhangers.
3. Build toward your midpoint and crisis.
4. Give the final stretch plenty of space to breathe.
5. Track your pages. Back up your work. Take a break.

CHAPTER 18
THE READY-TO-SHOOT PASS

GIVE THEM PAGES THEY CAN FILM TOMORROW

THIS IS THE MOMENT WHERE YOUR SCRIPT BECOMES **MARKET-READY**. Not perfect. **Shootable.** A producer should be able to open Episodes 1–50 and think: *We could film this tomorrow.* This pass ensures clarity, consistency, and production value. It is your final step before sending your script out for assignments.

MORNING: THE COMPLETE READ-THROUGH

Read your entire script start to finish without stopping. Don't edit yet. Just read and take notes.

What You're Looking For

1. Cliffhanger Effectiveness (Every Episode)

Go through Episodes 1–50 and rate each cliffhanger:

- **Strong:** Makes me need the next episode immediately
- **Okay:** Mild interest
- **Weak:** No urgency

Every "weak" or "okay" ending must be revised. Cliffhangers are your engine.

2. Character Voice Consistency

Track your protagonist first:

- Does their voice stay consistent from Episode 5 to Episode 45?
- Do they have phrases/speech patterns unique to them?

Track secondary characters:

- Can you tell who's speaking without the name?
- Does each character sound distinct?
- Mark any dialogue that feels "off."

3. Character Arc Tracking

Identify your protagonist's arc:

- **Episode 1:** Who they are, what they believe
- **Episode 20:** First test of that belief
- **Episode 40:** Forced to confront who they really are
- **Episode 50:** Who they've become

If the transformation isn't clear, mark episodes to strengthen.

4. Timeline Consistency

Watch for:

- Characters in two places at once
- Injuries that vanish
- Random weather flips
- Day/night continuity errors

- Mark anything that breaks logic.

CHARACTER DEVELOPMENT PRINCIPLES

The Want vs. Need Framework

Every protagonist has:

WANT (external):

- Revenge
- Prove themselves
- Win love
- Complete mission

NEED (internal):

- Forgive
- Trust
- Let go
- Accept themselves

Your series tracks the journey from WANT to NEED.

Character Consistency vs. Growth

Consistency:

- Speech
- Values
- Fears
- Humor

Growth:

- How they respond evolves
- Episode 1: Avoids conflict

- Episode 50: Faces it

They should feel like the same person, just transformed.

READ DIALOGUE ALOUD

Reading aloud reveals:

- Lines too long to speak
- Awkward phrasing
- Repetitive patterns
- Missing contractions
- Rhythm problems

If it's hard to say, it's hard to act.

Check your dialogue:

- Are characters stating emotions instead of revealing them through behavior?
- Is there subtext?
- Can you cut "I feel…" and show it instead?

CHARACTER-SPECIFIC SPEECH PATTERNS

Each character must have unique markers:

- one never swears, another swears constantly
- one uses questions, another statements
- one verbose, one clipped
- one direct, one evasive

Test: Cover the names. Can you tell who's speaking?

THE BRUTAL SCENE CUT

If you're over page count:

Ask of each episode:

"What is the ONE thing that must happen here?"

Keep that. Cut everything else.

CHARACTER CONSISTENCY CHECK

Physical Consistency

Track:

- Injuries
- Disabilities
- Hair/eye color
- Significant clothing
- Abilities/limitations

Emotional Consistency

If devastated in Episode 30, they can't be cheerful in Episode 31 without explanation.

Check transitions: If Episode 29 ends with tears, Episode 30 must reflect aftermath.

LOCATION & CHARACTER COUNT AUDIT

Count Your Locations

List every unique location.

Combine where possible.

Remember: Fewer locations = more producible = more likely to get hired.

Count Your Speaking Roles

- List every character with dialogue.
- Main cast: 2–3 characters
- Supporting: 3+ appearances

Try to keep total under **10 speaking roles**

Ask yourself:

- Can roles be combined?
- Can minor characters be silent?

READERS (YOUR QUALITY CONTROL)

Have someone read Episodes 1–5. Ask them:

- Did you want to keep reading?
- Which episode hooked you most?
- Was anything confusing?
- Did any dialogue feel unnatural?
- Could you distinguish characters?

If they aren't hooked by Episode 5, revise Episodes 1–5 before moving forward.

LAST CHECKS

- Correct names?
- Typos?
- Missing words?
- Repeated lines?
- Overlong action blocks?

When this pass is done, your script is no longer a draft, it's a professional, market-ready vertical series.

TAKE ACTION: STEP 18

1. Complete your read-through.
2. Rate all cliffhangers.
3. Strengthen character arcs.
4. Read every line aloud.
5. Trim scene fat.
6. Audit locations and cast for budget.
7. Polish your formatting.
8. Fix typos.

Your draft is now **Ready-to-Shoot,** and ready to send out for assignments.

CHAPTER 19
GETTING HIRED

STAND OUT, GET NOTICED, GET THE JOB

Most writers sit around waiting for opportunities to find them. Successful writers create their own. In the vertical space, work exists everywhere – but you must position yourself where producers can see you, hear you, and trust you.

This chapter shows you exactly where to look, how to apply, what to send, and how to build the relationships that lead to assignments.

SEIZE THE DAY: WHERE TO LOOK

1. LinkedIn Job Postings (Your #1 Source)

LinkedIn is the most active platform for vertical series writing jobs. Search terms:

- "Vertical series writer"
- "Short form content writer"
- "Microdrama writer"
- "ReelShort writer"
- "DramaBox writer"

Set job alerts:

- Daily notifications
- Apply immediately
- Introduce yourself

Who posts these jobs:

- Production companies
- Platforms
- Content studios
- Producers

2. Set Google Alerts (Your Automated Assistant)

Most writers forget this step. You shouldn't. Set Google Alerts for these keywords:

- "vertical series"
- "vertical drama"
- "microdrama"
- "short-form narrative"
- "ReelShort"
- "DramaBox"
- "short drama app"
- "portrait mode storytelling"

You'll automatically receive notifications whenever:

- New platform launches
- Studio announces a vertical division
- Producer is interviewed about verticals
- Job posting hits an obscure site
- Company mentions hiring writers
- Someone in the space posts an article

You become the first to know. And the writer with the most up-to-date intelligence is the writer who gets hired.

Set your alerts to:

Frequency: Once a day

Sources: News + Blogs + Web

Region: Any

This is quiet, passive networking, but extremely effective.

3. Writer Groups (Real-Time Intel)

- WhatsApp: The Hub-Verticals, also, VerticalsClub 9:16
- Facebook: Vertical Series Writers, Short Form Content Creators
- LinkedIn Groups + Discord servers with vertical channels
- Writers share jobs before they hit the public. Stay plugged in.

4. Production Companies (Go Straight to the Source)

Many vertical studios accept pitches or queries.

Research, find the submissions email, and reach out professionally.

Only send what they request.

5. Platforms (Occasional Direct Submissions)

Some apps offer creator portals.

Longer wait times, less common, still worth a shot.

THE APPLICATION PACKAGE

Your package should include:

- **Cover email** (short)
- **10-episode writing sample** (12–18 pages total)

- **Concept list** (10–20 ideas, each one paragraph)
- **Contact info and IMDb/portfolio**

But don't send anything without getting a request.

Why 10 Episodes Is the Magic Number

Producers need proof you understand:

- Episode 1: Hooks
- Episodes 2–9: Retain interest
- Episode 10: Delivers the paywall moment

10 episodes: Proof of vertical mastery.

THE COVER EMAIL THAT GETS OPENED

Subject: Vertical Series Writer – [Your Name]

Hi [Name],

I'm a vertical series writer specializing in [genre]. I understand the unique demands of the format: cliffhanger structure, 60–90 second pacing, and mobile-first storytelling.

If you have credits:

Recent work includes:

[Title] (60 episodes, [Platform], [Genre])*[Title]* (40 episodes, [Platform], [Genre])

If you don't have credits yet:

I've studied the format extensively and have a fully developed writing sample demonstrating vertical structure and pacing.

Attached:

- 10-episode writing sample (19 pages)

- Concept list (10–20 high-concept pitches)

I can deliver a complete 50–60 episode script in 10 days.

Happy to discuss your project.

Best,

[Name] [Phone] [Email] [IMDb] [LinkedIn]

Keep it short. They decide within **three seconds** whether to open attachments.

FOLLOWING UP (WITHOUT BEING ANNOYING)

Day 1: Apply

Day 7: One follow-up

Hi [Name],

Following up on my application for [position]. Let me know if you need anything else.

Thanks,

[Your Name]

Day 14: Move on. If they were interested, they would have responded.

Don't:

- Follow up more than once
- DM across multiple platforms
- Get emotional or pushy

Do:

- Apply for 20 others
- Build your portfolio
- Expand your network

DM STRATEGY (SUBTLE & EFFECTIVE)

When someone posts about a vertical series:

Their post: *"Wrapped filming my first vertical show!"*

Your DM:

Hi [Name],

Congrats on wrapping! (or whatever milestone they have reached) I'm a vertical series writer – who are you working with? Always looking to connect with producers in the space.

Thanks,

[Your Name]

This works because you're building a connection, not asking for a job.

RELATIONSHIPS FIRST, OPPORTUNITIES SECOND

Never lead with: "Can you hire me?"

Lead with:

- Curiosity about their work
- Support
- Useful sharing
- Value

Week 1: Comment on their posts

Week 2: Share something of theirs

Week 3: DM with a thoughtful comment

Week 4: Offer a useful link / resource

Week 5: Ask if they're hiring writers

By then, you're not a stranger. You're a colleague.

THE REFERRAL CHAIN

Most vertical assignments come from referrals.

How to get referred:

- Tell everyone you're looking
- Post openly about your work
- Refer others generously
- Thank people publicly

People remember writers who lift others up.

PRODUCER OUTREACH

Create a list of **50–100 producers** you know or want to know.

Sources include:

- Previous collaborators
- Film school or workshop connections
- Festival contacts
- LinkedIn connections of connections
- Producers whose work you admire

Assignments often come from the second-level network.

YOUR CONCEPT LIST

Your list = your ammo.

- You need **10–30 pitches**, each with:
- One-paragraph logline (55–75 words)
- Clear hook
- Clear stakes
- A twist

Make lists by genre:

- **List 1:** Romance (10 ideas)
- **List 2:** Thriller (7 ideas)
- **List 3:** Melodrama (7 ideas)

When a producer says "Got any thrillers?"

You send *exactly* what they want.

THE ONE-PAGE PITCH

For concepts gaining interest, have a clean one-pager:

- Title
- Genre | Episode Count
- Logline (50-70 words)
- Tone
- Synopsis (250-300 words)
- Character Breakdown
- Commercial Appeal
- Cliffhanger Highlights

One page total

THE PITCH DECK (OPTIONAL, IMPRESSIVE)

Use Canva or Google Slides.

Include:

- Title slide
- Who you are
- Market snapshot
- Concept slides (1 per slide)

AI imagery (Midjourney, DALL·E, SDXL) is a huge advantage.

COLLABORATION OPPORTUNITIES

Co-writing: Split episodes, split payment

Writers' rooms: 3–4 writers, faster delivery

Mentorship: Junior writer drafts, senior writer polishes

HOW TO BECOME THE WRITER EVERYONE REFERS

- Deliver early
- Take notes well
- Make producer's job easy
- Communicate clearly
- Deliver clean drafts

If you're professional and fast, producers will tell other producers about you.

RED FLAGS – RUN!

- Producers asking for free work
- Requests for full scripts without agreements
- No clear terms
- Too-good-to-be-true promises
- No written contract
- Payment far below market
- Bad reputation
- Something feels off
- Trust your gut.

There are plenty of legitimate opportunities.

TRACKING YOUR PITCHES

Spreadsheet columns:

- Producer
- Date contacted
- Concepts pitched
- Response
- Follow-up date
- Status

Why this matters:

- Avoid pitching the same concept twice
- Know when to follow up
- Track which ideas get traction

THE BOTTOM LINE

Getting hired is **active**, not passive.

- Apply everywhere.
- Reach out.
- Be visible.
- Be generous.
- Deliver excellence.

Producers need writers who can deliver vertical scripts fast, professionally, and with commercial hooks.

Be that writer.

TAKE ACTION: STEP 19

This week:

1. Identify 5 producers you want to work with

2. Research them
3. Send personalized outreach emails
4. Build your concept list (10–30 ideas)
5. Polish your 10-episode writing sample
6. Set up LinkedIn job alerts
7. Join The Hub Verticals WhatsApp group and introduce yourself

You are not "hoping" to get hired. You are taking steps to get hired.

CHAPTER 20
ASSIGNMENT TIMELINE

YOU GOT THE JOB! NOW WHAT?

UNDERSTANDING THE VERTICAL SERIES WRITING PROCESS

Vertical assignments move fast, and slow, at the same time. Fast when you're writing. Slow when you're waiting. Here's the real workflow behind most professional vertical series jobs.

THE DEVELOPMENT PHASE

Day 1: Concept Development

You and the producer align on:

- Core idea
- Trope
- Genre
- Main conflict
- Hook
- Paywall reveal direction

You pitch your take. They approve it. You move forward.

Days 2–4: Outline

You outline the full series (Episodes 1-50 or 1-60 depending on project). Your outline is your blueprint, this is where the real thinking happens.

Feedback / Waiting

You submit your outline. The producer reviews it.

This can take:

- 48 hours
- 5 days
- 2 weeks

All normal.

Days 5–9: First Draft

Once the outline is approved, you write. Vertical writing is fast and intense:

- 10 episodes a day
- 5–6 pages a day
- 50–60 episodes completed in under a week

You stay focused. You stay consistent. You keep your cliffhangers sharp.

Day 10: Polish Pass

Before delivering:

- Strengthen cliffhangers
- Clean dialogue
- Fix logic gaps

- Tighten pacing
- Trim unnecessary action lines

Deliver

You submit a professional, polished draft. This is your "ready-to-shoot" version.

THE REVISION PHASE

Waiting for Notes

Producers can take days or weeks. Don't panic. Don't interrupt. This is normal.

Addressing Notes

Once you receive notes:

2-3 days to execute revisions

1 day for any final tweaks

Revisions are part of the job. Your attitude toward notes is what gets you rehired.

More Waiting

Producer reviews your revision. Sometimes there's one more round. Sometimes it's approved immediately.

Pre-Production Begins

Once the script is locked, production moves into:

- Casting
- Locations
- Scheduling

- Shot lists
- Blocking
- Budgeting

Your job shifts to availability for clarifications.

WHAT THIS MEANS FOR YOU

The writing is fast. The waiting is unpredictable.

You might hear back in:

- 24-48 hours, or
- 10-14 days

Both are normal in this industry.

Every Writer Has a Different Rhythm

Some writers can:

- Outline in 2 days
- Write 10 episodes in 1 day
- Polish in a few hours

Others require:

- 4-5 days to outline
- 3 days to write 10 episodes
- More breathing room

Both are fine, **as long as you know your pace.**

WHY KNOWING YOUR PACE MATTERS

When a producer asks: **"How long will this take you?"**

Your answer must be:

- Honest
- Precise
- Reliable

If you say 10 days but need 15:

- You'll miss deadlines
- Lose trust
- Jeopardize future jobs

If you say 15 days but could do 10:

- You may lose the job to someone faster.
- This industry rewards reliability.

Producers need writers who say what they can do and deliver it.

WHAT YOU CAN CONTROL

- The speed of your revision turnaround
- The quality of your pages
- Clear communication about timeline
- Your reliability
- Your attitude toward notes

WHAT YOU CANNOT CONTROL

- Locking an outline
- How long producers take to review
- Whether they deliver one round of notes or three
- When pre-production begins
- Internal platform deadlines

- Professionalism = **mastering your part and being flexible with theirs.**

THE PROFESSIONAL APPROACH

- Know your real speed
- Communicate clearly
- Deliver when you say you will
- Stay available for notes
- Be patient
- Never complain publicly
- Your reliability is as important as your writing.

TAKE ACTION: STEP 20

1. Track your time for each phase as you move through this workbook.
2. Concept development days
3. Outline days
4. Writing speed (Episodes 1-10, 11-50)
5. Polish duration
6. Know your numbers.

So when a producer asks: **"How fast can you deliver?"** You can answer with confidence, not hope.

You are now ready for the development process.

CHAPTER 21
THE DEVELOPMENT PROCESS

SHOW THEM YOU'RE NOT JUST A WRITER — YOU'RE A PRO

VERTICAL SERIES WRITING IS COLLABORATIVE FROM DAY ONE. UNLIKE traditional screenwriting where a writer completes a full draft alone before anyone sees it, vertical writing begins with alignment. You will meet with producers, directors, and often platform representatives before you craft your outline.

This chapter teaches you how to collaborate like a professional, how to navigate conflicting notes, and how to build relationships that lead to ongoing assignments.

THE CREATIVE MEETING

Your creative meeting sets the vision for the entire project. This meeting defines the story, the tone, the resources, the cast, and the overall production plan. A clear meeting upfront prevents major issues later.

WHO IS IN THE ROOM OR ZOOM

You may meet with any combination of the following:

Producer: Controls budget, resources, casting, and the relationship with the platform. Final say on business decisions.

Director: Understands what can be filmed quickly and efficiently. Ensures your script is producible within the schedule and available locations.

Writer (You): Responsible for the story structure, character arcs, dialogue, and emotional pacing. Your job is to make the series gripping and producible.

Client or Brand Representative: If the series is sponsored or branded, the client may attend to ensure brand alignment. They may have key requirements regarding themes, representation, or messaging.

Platform Representative: If the project is for a specific app, a platform rep may attend to clarify tone, tropes, content restrictions, viewer preferences, or specific mandates for the app.

Story Editor or Executive Producer: Some companies include a story editor or senior producer to help shape the creative direction.

Your job as the writer is to listen, ask the right questions, and clarify everything before you outline.

WHAT THE CREATIVE MEETING COVERS

1. Genre and Tone

Everyone must be aligned on:

- Genre
- Sub-genre
- Tonal palette
- Pacing
- Comparable vertical shows or films for the vibe

You want everyone watching the same show in their mind.

2. Locations and Resources

Ask:

- What locations do we have
- What rooms or areas within those locations
- How many days and hours we have access
- Any limitations (noise, lighting, neighbors, time windows)

Your story must match what can actually be filmed.

3. Cast Size and Budget Parameters

Ask:

- How many characters
- How many supporting characters
- Special requirements or limitations (limited hours, minors, stunts)
- Cast size impacts character arcs, storytelling complexity, and scene count.

4. Story Concept and Core Conflict

Clarify:

- Who is the protagonist?
- What they want?
- What stands in their way?
- Who the key relationship is?
- What emotional journey the story explores?
- What the major turning points are?

You need a clear emotional spine before you outline.

5. Episode Count and Target Length

Ask:

- How many episodes?
- Target duration per episode?
- Total length of the series?
- Any special timing requirements for cliffhangers?

This determines pacing and how deep your arcs can go.

6. Platform or Client Requirements

If the project involves a platform rep or a client, ask:

- Any content restrictions
- Tropes that perform well on the app
- Elements the client requires
- Prohibited material
- Cultural sensitivities
- Specific audience demographics

This prevents costly rewrites later.

BY THE END OF THE MEETING YOU SHOULD KNOW

This step is highly recommended.

- What was discussed?
- What was agreed on?
- The outline deadline.
- The script deadline.
- Who approves what?
- Any unresolved questions.
- The next steps.

- Platform or client expectations.
- Outline deadline.
- Draft deadline.
- Who has final approval?

You would be surprised how often people leave a meeting with different interpretations. Your email ensures everyone is aligned. It also protects you if someone later forgets what they approved.

Never leave a meeting with assumptions. Ask until you have clarity.

AFTER THE MEETING: SEND A CONFIRMATION EMAIL

After the meeting, send a short email to everyone recapping everything.

WORKING WITH DIRECTORS FROM THE BEGINNING

In vertical series, the director is not someone who receives the script after you are done.

They are involved from the very beginning because:

- They know what is shootable
- They know how many setups can be done in a day
- They understand the limitations of the location
- They know what the cast can realistically perform
- They know the look and tone the production wants

If a director says something will not work practically, believe them. Adjust early. Collaboration avoids costly rewrites and strengthens your script.

WHEN SOMEONE PITCHES AN OFF-TONE OR INAPPROPRIATE IDEA

Creative rooms move fast. Occasionally someone may pitch something that is:

- Off-tone
- Against platform rules
- Questionable ethically or creatively
- Inconsistent with the story
- Inappropriate (Example: A bizarre suggestion that sexualizes a character or crosses boundaries)

Handle it with professionalism, but respect your boundaries.

Redirect with clarity: "That might be too intense for the tone we established. What if we explore a version that keeps the stakes high but aligns with the platform guidelines."

or

"I think the emotional impact is right, but we might need another approach that fits the audience expectations better."

Offer an alternative that meets the same goal without breaking the project.

CONFLICTING NOTES

Sometimes different people give contradictory notes.

If this happens:

- Identify who has final authority
- Address both concerns when possible
- Offer solutions, not resistance
- Reframe the conversation around story goals
- Clarify decisions in writing afterward

Diplomacy is part of the job.

SIGNS OF A HEALTHY COLLABORATION

- Clear authority
- Notes with reasoning
- Decisions that stick
- Respectful communication
- Realistic timelines
- Clear resource lists
- Alignment on tone and story

RED FLAGS THAT MEAN YOU SHOULD WALK AWAY

- Chaotic vision that changes constantly
- Major budget cuts with unchanged expectations
- Disrespectful behavior toward you
- Refusal to give clear approvals
- Unrealistic deadlines with no flexibility
- A pattern of non-payment or delayed payment

Your career is built on reliability and professionalism, not self-sacrifice.

HOW TO BUILD RELATIONSHIPS THAT LEAD TO REPEAT WORK

- Deliver on time or early
- Take notes gracefully
- Write producible, tight, emotional pages
- Be easy to communicate with
- Stay in touch after production wraps
- Celebrate the project when it releases
- Support producers and directors publicly

- Refer opportunities to others

When people like working with you, they bring you back. Often again and again.

TAKE ACTION: STEP 21

- Track every creative meeting in a document
- Note who attends, who approves, and the deadlines
- Send a follow-up email after every meeting
- Keep all notes organized
- Confirm all next steps in writing
- Build collaborative habits that make producers trust you

Become the writer everyone wants to hire again.

CHAPTER 22
WRITING FOR A BUDGET

WRITE IT SO THEY CAN AFFORD TO MAKE IT

THE MOST HIREABLE WRITERS UNDERSTAND PRODUCTION REALITY BEFORE they start writing. You can write the most brilliant vertical series, but if it is not producible on a $150K budget, producers cannot shoot it. Your goal is not only to write a great story but to write a great story that fits the production model.

Note: Every production company works slightly differently. This chapter outlines the most accurate portrait of a typical $150K vertical series production. Use these guidelines, not absolute rules.

THE $150K BUDGET REALITY

A standard vertical series budget around $150K typically includes:

- **Shooting schedule:** 6 to 9 days.
- **Cast:** Non-union actors. 6 to 10 speaking roles.
- **Locations:** 3 to 5 primary locations. Used again and again, sometimes redressed to appear different.
- **Crew:** Small team. People often handle multiple duties.
- **Post-production:** 2 to 3 weeks. Fast turnaround.
- **Complexity:** Minimal. No VFX. No stunts. No elaborate setups. No expensive props. No big wardrobe changes.

This is the reality you write for.

WHAT TO WRITE

Interior locations: Interiors are cheaper and easier than exteriors.

Examples:

- INT. APARTMENT
- INT. BEDROOM
- INT. OFFICE
- INT. COFFEE SHOP

Why: No weather issues, no permits, simpler lighting.

Small cast in each scene: Two to four characters per scene.

Why: Actors cost money. Fewer actors = lower cost.

Dialogue-driven conflict: Arguments, emotional confrontations, confessions, romantic tension, secrets revealed.

Why: Dialogue is free. Emotional drama is free. Explosions are not.

Reusable locations

- The same house, office, or villa can play:
- Bedroom
- Office
- Restaurant
- Hotel lobby
- AirBnB

With minimal redressing.

Contemporary settings: Modern wardrobe, no special props, no period detail.

Emotional stories: Family tension, forbidden romance, crime drama, betrayal, jealousy, ambition, secrets.

WHAT NOT TO WRITE

You can include one or two of these only if the producer approves and only if essential to the story.

- **Crowd scenes:** Weddings, parties, bars with extras.
- **Car chases or vehicle action:** Driving scenes, crashes, chase sequences.
- **Stunts or complex fights:** Anything more than simple pushing or grabbing requires a stunt coordinator.
- **Frequent costume changes:** Keep wardrobe minimal and repeatable.
- **Travel-based stories:** Scripts that take place in multiple cities or exotic locations.
- **VFX or supernatural CGI:** Unless the platform specifically wants it, avoid.
- **Children under 12:** Strict labor laws, required guardian, limited hours.
- **Animals:** Trainers and animal unpredictability increase time and cost.
- **Night exterior scenes:** Night lighting is expensive and slow.

The rule: Always write with the shoot in mind.

THE "I HAVE A VILLA" CONVERSATION

One of the most common things you will hear from producers is, "I have access to a villa. Can we set the series there?"

This is normal. In vertical series:

- Free locations are gold
- Shooting in one place saves thousands
- No permits needed
- Crew never moves
- Cast stays in one place

Your answer: "Absolutely. What kind of villa? How many rooms are available to us?"

Then craft a story built around that location.

The same happens with:

- Warehouses
- Offices
- Restaurants
- Beach houses
- Lofts
- Cabins

A skilled vertical writer knows how to wrap a compelling story around ANY location.

WHY CONSTRAINTS MAKE YOUR STORY BETTER

The fewer choices you have, the more focused your story becomes. Without constraints: The story could be set anywhere, which often leads to paralysis. With constraints: You write tight, specific, high-stakes stories that feel intentional.

Examples of stories that thrive in one location:

- **Romance:** Two rivals hired to plan a wedding at a villa.
- **Thriller:** A billionaire invites strangers to his villa for a job interview. One winds up dead.
- **Melodrama:** Three sisters must live together for 30 days or lose their inheritance.

Constraints force ingenuity and depth.

THE 6 TO 9 DAY SHOOT (MOSTLY 6)

This is incredibly fast. Traditional TV shoots 5 to 8 pages per day. Vertical series shoots 10 to 15 pages per day.

Why so fast?

- Limited budget
- Minimal lighting setups
- Fewer locations
- One main cast
- Mobile-first simple coverage

What this means for your writing:

- Keep scenes simple
- Avoid complex blocking
- Dialogue should be direct and playable
- Minimal props
- Minimal physicality
- Emotion-driven beats over action beats

The simpler the setup, the more takes the director can get. More takes equals better acting.

REDUCED LOCATIONS

Where productions once struggled to find affordable spaces, **dedicated vertical studios** are now opening across the country, especially in Los Angeles.

These studios offer:

- Multiple ready-to-shoot standing sets
- Apartments and luxury penthouses
- Hospitals and exam rooms
- Police stations and interrogation rooms
- Offices and conference rooms
- Restaurants, cafés, and bars
- Classrooms and hallways
- Mansions and estate interiors
- Hotels, lobbies, and stairwells

Many facilities now have **multiple sets under one roof**, designed specifically for fast-paced microdrama production.

But the rule for writers stays the same.

Even with all these new spaces, each additional location still:

- Adds lighting changes
- Adds blocking adjustments
- Adds setup / reset time
- Slows down production
- Increases cost

Most vertical productions shoot **10-15 pages per day**, and that pace depends on **contained, efficient writing**.

THE GOLDEN RULE

Keep it to 5-7 locations.

Producers love scripts that:

- Film fast
- Reduce transitions
- Take full advantage of studio sets
- Minimize company moves

Maximize time spent on performance and cinematography

WRITE SMART FOR THE NEW STUDIO ERA

You can safely write scenes set in:

- A living room
- A bedroom
- A kitchen
- An office

- A hospital room
- A hallway
- A restaurant interior
- These sets exist in every major vertical studio.

Avoid overcomplicating your script with:

- Frequent new locations
- Hard-to-find environments
- Exterior-heavy storytelling

Places requiring permits or special access

THE TRUTH IS

The studios make things easier. They're built to increase production value, not increase production complexity.

CAST SIZE: THE SIX CHARACTER GUIDELINE

Ideal cast size:

- Protagonist
- Love interest or antagonist
- Best friend or confidant
- Rival or complication
- Authority figure
- Wild card or twist character
- Plus a few day players.

This keeps the budget manageable and the story intimate.

WHAT DIRECTORS NEED FROM YOU

Directors read your script asking:

"Can I shoot this in 7 days without breaking the schedule or budget?"

You help them say yes by writing:

- Clear action
- Simple setups
- Limited locations
- Two-person scenes
- Dialogue that flows
- Strong emotional turns
- Minimal props
- No stunts or VFX unless approved

TAKE ACTION: STEP 22

1. Count your locations. Aim for 3 to 5.
2. Count your characters. Aim for 6 core characters.
3. Eliminate expensive elements like crowds, stunts, animals, children, travel, VFX, or night exteriors.
4. If a producer says they have a villa, warehouse, office, or restaurant, practice mapping your story inside that space.
5. Reread your outline through a budget lens.
6. Ask yourself: Could this truly be filmed in 6 to 9 days?

Your script does not need to feel small. It needs to feel intentional, emotional, and producible.

CHAPTER 23
SEND, INVOICE, REPEAT

HOW TO STAY BOOKED, BUSY, AND PAID

ONE LAST CHECK

Do one last read-through. No rewriting. No big changes. Just catch the obvious things.

Look for:

- Character name misspellings
- Inconsistent location names
- Missing scene headings
- Dialogue attribution errors
- Homophone errors (your/you're, its/it's)
- Episode numbering issues

Do not rewrite at this stage. This is a surface check, nothing more.

FILE FORMAT & NAMING

Before you export, check what your producer asked for:

- PDF (most common)
- Final Draft (.fdx)

- Sometimes both

File naming convention:

YourName_SeriesTitle_Draft_Date.pdf

Example: Drean_BlindDesire_Draft2_Nov09.pdf

COVER PAGE REQUIREMENTS

Include:

- Title
- Your name
- Contact info
- Draft number and date
- Episode count and page count

Example:

BLIND BRIDE: 60 Episodes / 88 Pages / Written by Isabel Dréan

Draft 2 – May 9, 2025

Contact: isabel@isabeldrean.com | (555) 123-4567

THE SUBMISSION EMAIL

Keep it brief, clean, and professional.

Subject: Series Title – Final Draft Submission

Hi [Producer Name],

Attached is the final draft of **[Series Title]**:

[Episode count] episodes

[Page count] pages

All notes from [date] incorporated

Per your specs: [File format] attached

[Any additional requirements they mentioned]

I'm available for any further adjustments or questions.

Thank you for the opportunity to work on this project.

Best,

[Your Name][Phone][Email]

Don't:

- Apologize
- Justify choices
- Explain your process
- Ask if they "liked it"
- Add unnecessary fluff

Do:

- Confirm requirements
- Stay available
- Keep it professional

YOU DELIVERED — NOW REWARD YOURSELF

You just delivered a full vertical series. That's huge. Celebrate. Rest. Step away from your screen. This is part of the process.

UNDERSTANDING THE COLLABORATIVE PROCESS

Your script is the blueprint, not the final product.

Vertical series pipeline:

Writer → Script Producer → Director → Actors → Editor → Platform

Each person transforms your work. That means:

- Scenes may be cut
- Dialogue may change
- Actors interpret lines differently
- Editors restructure moments

The final released version will differ from your script. Make peace with this now.

FOLLOW-UP COMMUNICATION

What happens after you deliver:

- Immediate approval (rare but amazing)
- Minor tweaks
- More notes
- Silence (it's normal, they're reviewing)

When to check in:

48 hours: Light follow-up

5 business days: Second follow-up

7+ days: Move on. They may be paused

(Do *not* message every day. Professional patience matters.)

INVOICE & PAYMENT

Always know payment terms BEFORE writing. If contract says payment on delivery, send your invoice the same day as the final draft.

Include:

- Your name + contact
- Invoice number
- Date

- Project title
- Amount due
- Payment terms
- Banking/Pay details
- Track everything.

NEXT: DON'T WAIT

The minute you hit send… start lining up the next job.

Ways to do that:

- **Leverage the project you just finished:** "Just wrapped a 60-episode vertical series for [Producer]. Open for new assignments."
- **Reach out to past and new producers:** Short, friendly, proactive emails.
- **Post on social media:** You're signaling availability.
- **Build 5–10 new concepts:** So you always have pitches ready.
- **Stay active in vertical communities:** WhatsApp, Facebook, Discord, LinkedIn groups.

Momentum is built by staying visible.

BUILDING YOUR VERTICAL PORTFOLIO

After 2–3 projects: Update your website and materials.

After 5+ projects: You're a recognized specialist. At that point, producers often approach you first.

THE PRODUCTION REALITY

- Unlike TV, you are rarely involved after delivery.
- Directors might ask a question or two
- You might provide a tweak during shooting
- Final edit may shift structure or lines

- Expect changes and embrace them
- Your work is done. Let the team do theirs.

WHEN YOUR SERIES RELEASES

- Promote it.
- Celebrate the team.
- Share links.
- Be positive.
- Do **not** publicly criticize edits or changes.

Professionalism buys you your next job.

THE HARD TRUTH

- Not every script gets produced.
- Projects pause.
- Budgets change.
- Platforms shift priorities.

This is normal. Your job is to keep pitching, keep writing, and keep building relationships. Consistency wins.

TAKE ACTION: STEP 23

1. Deliver your script, clean and professional
2. Submit your invoice
3. Celebrate
4. Begin outreach for the next project
5. Build new concepts
6. Keep your momentum going

You wrote a vertical series. Now it's time to leverage it into your next assignment.

CHAPTER 24
GETTING NOTES

IT'S NOT PERSONAL

You have submitted your polished draft. Now comes the part that separates professionals from amateurs: how you handle feedback. Every writer gets notes.

The writers who build long careers are the ones who handle notes well. This part of the vertical series industry expects fast turnaround and clean execution. But fast does not mean rushing or overpromising. Fast means efficient. Fast means organized. Fast means reliable.

Your goal is simple: take notes without resistance, execute them with clarity, and deliver on time.

THE GOLDEN RULE: GO LIMP

The best mindset for receiving notes is this: Remove all resistance.

When you get notes from a producer, your instinct will be to defend your choices, explain your reasoning, or argue why the change is unnecessary. Do not do this.

Go limp.

Like a rag doll. Accept the notes without resistance. Take a moment and return when you're ready. Your job is not to protect your vision. Your job is to solve the problems the producer identifies.

Why this approach works:

- You get hired again
- Revisions move quickly
- You become known as easy to work with
- You learn what producers actually need
- You stay employed

Your mantra is simple: **Understood. I will revise immediately.**

WHAT IS NEGOTIABLE VS. NOT

Most notes are not negotiable.

When you receive notes, assume everything is required unless they explicitly say otherwise. Common note categories that are never negotiable:

Budget and Production Constraints

- Cut night scenes
- Reduce locations
- Remove a character
- No children under five
- No animals
- No stunts
- Only one exterior location

Platform or Format Requirements

- Page count must be under the limit
- Episode 10 cliffhanger must be bigger

- Too many episodes are too long
- Need more conflict early

Story and Character Notes

- Protagonist feels passive
- A character vanishes for too many episodes
- The big reveal does not land
- Emotional stakes are too low

Content and Rating Notes

- Remove explicit content
- Reduce violence
- Avoid stereotypes (if you can - they usually love them)
- Adjust tone to platform guidelines

For all of these, the correct response is: **Understood. I will revise immediately.**

WHEN YOU CAN PUSH BACK

You get one pushback per project. Maybe.

Only use it if the note:

- Breaks core story logic
- Makes the show impossible to tell
- Violates basic ethics
- Creates harm or misrepresentation

If you must push back, do it this way:

"I understand the concern. What if we try this alternative that solves the issue and keeps the character consistent?"

Never:

"That does not work. " "I disagree."

Always offer a solution, not resistance. But truly: save your pushback for emergencies. Ninety-nine percent of notes are better solved than debated.

THE OUTLINE PRINCIPLE

If your outline was approved, you should get light notes on the script. Approved outline equals:

- Structure approved
- Arcs approved
- Tone approved
- Story beats approved
- Notes at the draft stage should be refinements such as:
- Tighten pacing
- Strengthen cliffhanger
- Cut a few pages
- Adjust a location for budget
- If you get major notes like:
- Change the ending
- Remove ten episodes
- Add a new love interest

One of three things happened:

- The outline was never truly approved
- The producer changed their mind
- The script deviated from the outline

Regardless, your job stays the same:

Go limp. Make the changes.

WHEN NOTES CROSS ETHICAL LINES

This is the one area where you should speak up immediately. If a note encourages:

1. Romanticizing abuse or assault

"Make the assault scene sexier."

Your response: "I am not comfortable sexualizing assault. What if we create tension through emotional stakes instead?"

2. Removing consent

"He should take charge without asking."

Your response: "I would like to keep consent clear. It is important to me and to the audience."

3. Harmful stereotypes

"Make the Asian character better at math."

Your response: "I prefer to avoid stereotypes. What if we give them a unique skill that supports the story?"

4. Weakening female characters

"She should need rescuing more."

Your response: "That undercuts her arc. What if they support each other?"

If the producer insists, you have options:

- Make the change if you can live with it
- Withdraw if your contract allows
- Complete the job and never use it as a sample

Until the vertical market matures and we improve how women are depicted within these stories, you will occasionally receive notes that cross ethical lines.

Unfortunately, this is still common in the early stages of a growing industry. You have to decide what you are willing to accept.

HOW TO REVISE EFFICIENTLY

Step 1: Read all notes without reacting

Do not start revising. Read everything once.

Step 2: Categorize

Mark each note as:

QUICK: Typo, trim line, minor adjustment

MEDIUM: Rewrite a scene, add emotion, strengthen cliffhanger

BIG: Cut character, restructure episodes, change location strategy

Step 3: Create a revision plan

Start with BIG notes. They influence everything else.

Step 4: Execute systematically

- Big changes
- Medium rewrites
- Quick fixes
- Do not jump around randomly.

Step 5: Proofread before sending

Give yourself at least one fresh read.

Step 6: Deliver on time

Never late. Never sloppy.

TURNAROUND TIMES

Typical timelines for vertical series:

- Light notes: 1 to 2 days
- Medium notes: 3 to 4 days
- Heavy notes: 5 to 7 days
- Full restructuring: up to 10 days

Never promise a timeline just to impress someone. Promise the timeline you can deliver.

Producers prefer a writer who says four days and delivers in three over a writer who says two days and delivers in five.

SCENE ECONOMY PRINCIPLES

Vertical series must move fast. Use these rules:

One episode equals one major beat

- Reveal information
- Shift a relationship
- Increase danger
- Force a choice
- Sharpen tension

If an episode tries to do more than one thing, split it.

Cut to the chase

Start scenes late. End them early.

Cut:

- Small talk
- Repetitive set-up
- Unnecessary transitions

Keep:

- Essential beat
- Visual action
- Emotional reaction

Every action line must matter

Each line should:

- Advance the plot
- Reveal character
- Build cliffhanger

If it does none of these, remove it.

PACING PRINCIPLES

Vertical episodes must feel like momentum.

Episode timing:

- 2 to 2 pages
- 1 to 3 scenes
- Ideally one scene per episode

Episodes 1 to 20: Build world and tension

Episodes 21 to 40: Escalate rapidly

Episodes 41 to 50: Push through climax

Each episode should feel faster than the one before it.

ONE ROUND OF NOTES (USUALLY)

Most vertical series go through:

- Notes on the outline
- Notes on the script
- Lock
- Move to production

You usually get one round. This is not traditional TV. There is no room for four rounds. Get it right the first time.

TAKE ACTION: STEP 24

1. Read notes without reacting
2. Categorize by scope
3. Create a revision plan
4. Execute efficiently
5. Communicate your timeline clearly
6. Deliver on time
7. Make revisions fast and clean
8. Maintain professionalism throughout

You are becoming the kind of writer producers rehire again and again.

CHAPTER 25
CONTRACTS & MONEY

GET THE BAG WITHOUT SELLING YOUR SOUL

DISCLOSURE: I'm not an attorney. Nothing in this chapter is legal advice. When in doubt, consult an entertainment lawyer.

Let's talk about money. The version where you pay rent, eat food, support your family, and build a career.

UNDERSTANDING WORK-FOR-HIRE

What You're Giving Up

A standard vertical series contract is *work-for-hire*.

This means the producer owns:

- The story concept
- The characters
- All dialogue and plot points
- Sequels or spinoffs
- Adaptations (book, feature film, TV)
- Everything (Hopefully this will change in the future)

What You Keep

- Your payment
- Credit (if negotiated)
- The right to say "I wrote this"
- The ability to describe the project in your portfolio

This is non-negotiable 99 percent of the time. You own nothing. You get paid once. Make peace with this before entering the space.

CURRENT RATES (2025)

Average range: **$2,000–$7,000 per 60-episode script**.

Rates have tripled since early 2024 and continue to rise.

Your First Series

For your first vertical series, you may accept a lower rate to get a produced credit. A produced credit is worth more long term than the immediate fee.

After your first produced credit:

- Set your minimum.
- Stick to it.

But if you want to develop a new relationship with an app or a producer, sometimes you have to be more flexible.

Prioritize Producers Who:

- Have a track record of releasing series
- Move fast (script to release in 4–8 weeks)
- Pay on time

VOLUME ECONOMICS: WHY THIS MODEL WORKS

Traditional TV writer: 1–2 episodes per year, higher rate, residuals.

Vertical series writer: 12–24 series per year, lower per-project rate, no residuals, but constant work.

This is a *volume business*. When you write fast, stay consistent, and build credits, the math works extremely well.

WHAT'S INCLUDED IN YOUR FEE

Every producer is different. But here is a standard deliverable package:

- Outline + 2 rounds of notes
- Full draft + 1 round of notes + 1 round of light notes

Critical: Once the outline is approved, no major story changes. Lock structure early.

Don't Overdeliver

If you're being paid $2K, don't do four rounds of notes.

- Set boundaries:
- How many revisions are included?
- What counts as "major changes?"
- What is "light notes?"

Standard: **1–2 rounds maximum**.

What's NOT Included (unless you negotiate it):

- Unlimited rewrites
- Consulting during production
- Marketing or social media support

- Writing additional episodes
- Sequels or spinoffs

NEVER START WITHOUT A WRITTEN CONTRACT

- Minimum contract must include:
- Names of both parties
- Project title
- Scope of work (60-episode script)
- Total fee
- Payment schedule
- Delivery timeline
- Revision policy
- Ownership (work-for-hire)
- Credit terms
- Payment method

If they say, *"Let's start now and do paperwork later,"* respond:

"I'm excited to begin! I'll start as soon as we have the signed agreement."

Do not budge on this.

PREDATORY BEHAVIOR EXISTS

Protect yourself:

- Ask other writers about producers
- Join vertical communities (WhatsApp, FB, LinkedIn, Discord)
- Share information about who pays and who doesn't
- Speak up when producers behave badly
- Your best protection is community.

COMMON SCAMS (AND YOUR RESPONSE)

- **Write a few episodes to prove yourself.** → I don't write spec work.
- **We'll pay once it's produced.** → I'm paid upon delivery.
- **It's great exposure!**→ Exposure doesn't pay my bills. My fee is $___.
- **Endless rounds of notes.** → Additional revisions are a separate fee.
- **Concept theft.** → Include this in every pitch email: *These concepts are proprietary and cannot be used without a signed agreement.*
- **Optional-step contracts.** They pay $500 for your concept and then ditch you. → Walk away.
- **No contract necessary.** → Absolutely not.
- **We'll pay after platform approval.**→ That could be never. Decline.

VET THE PRODUCER BEFORE YOU SIGN

- Google them
- Ask other writers
- Check their produced content
- Ask for references
- Trust your instincts

If something feels off, it probably is.

THE SELF-PROTECTION CHECKLIST

Before starting:

- Signed contract
- Fair payment schedule
- Clear revision policy

- Verified producer reputation
- Confirmed payment method
- Confirmed credit terms
- Gut feeling is positive

If you can't check most boxes, reconsider the job.

PROTECTING YOUR PITCHES

You can't fully protect ideas. The vertical space is still the Wild West. Add this line to pitch emails:

These concepts are proprietary and cannot be used without a signed agreement.

It's not bulletproof, but it's something. Your real protection is speed and volume.

CREDIT

If they offer IMDb credit, take it. It matters for future work.

PREFERRED PAYMENT SCHEDULE

A simple, fair payment structure protects you and keeps the work moving without delays. The cleanest schedule, and the one I prefer, is:

50 percent upon delivery of the first draft:

You've done the bulk of the work. You deserve to be paid for it.

50 percent upon approval of the final draft:

Notes, polish, and delivery.

This keeps everything streamlined and eliminates a situation where you're doing multiple unpaid steps before receiving your first payment.

A three-step payment schedule also works well:

- Upon delivery of the outline
- Upon delivery of the first draft
- Upon approval of the final draft

This is common in traditional TV and film — but here's the rule you MUST remember:

If they want to own your work after the outline, that is unacceptable.

An outline is not a script. It is not the full value of your creative labor.

And handing over ownership at that stage leaves you exposed, underpaid, and replaceable.

Payment schedules should support your work — not exploit it.

WHEN PRODUCERS DON'T PAY

If a payment is past due, follow a clear, professional timeline:

Day 5 past due: Polite reminder

Day 10 past due: Firmer reminder

Day 15 past due: Final notice

Day 20+: Small claims + privately warn your peers

Keep EVERYTHING: contracts, invoices, emails, text messages.

But here's the part no one tells you:

Some producers are extremely hands-on and do not have an accountant on staff. If they are actively in production, they might literally be on set fourteen hours a day with no manpower to process payments.

If they are established, reputable, and responsive, **be patient** — they will pay you once they're out of the production chaos.

Just learn to tell the difference:

Busy is fine.

Avoidant is not.

And unpaid labor is never part of the job.

RIGHTS & IP

Most vertical series work is:

- Work-for-hire
- No rights retained
- No residuals
- No backend

As of now, this is standard. 99 percent of the time you cannot reuse or resell anything. Hopefully this will change with time.

THE WGA AND MICRODRAMAS (2025)

WGA *can* cover vertical work, but:

- Few producers are signatories
- Joining prematurely limits your opportunities
- Build credits now while non-union work is abundant

CONTRACT REVIEW

ALWAYS READ YOUR CONTRACT

Always read every single word of your contract. Slow down. Take your time. If you can hire an attorney, do it. Nothing protects you better.

When the pay is low and you can't justify legal fees, I run the contract through ChatGPT and ask for red flags. It's surprisingly good at spotting the clauses that could hurt you later. Use every tool you have. Protect your work. Protect yourself. Use an attorney for high-paying gigs.

Red flags:

- Optional steps
- Unlimited revisions
- No clear payment timeline
- Non-compete clauses
- No guaranteed credit
- Payment only if produced

NEGOTIATION TRICK

Producer: **What's your rate?**

Your answer: **What's the budget for the writer?**

Make *them* say the number first. I was always told the first person who says a number in a negotiation loses. Not sure if that's true but I don't risk it.

WHEN TO SPEAK UP

If a producer doesn't pay: **Warn the community.** Discreetly. There are many groups and forums and warning lists are starting to appear. Writers need to protect each other against predatory behavior.

REAL TALK

Listen, it is the wild west out here. Navigating this industry in any format is a challenge. You get dragged along thinking a deal is coming and then you are ghosted.

- You prepare pitch after pitch just to book one gig.
- The pay does not always feel adequate.
- The timelines are chaotic.
- People change their minds.
- Platforms shift priorities overnight.

It is what it is. If you cannot face those challenges, if you need things to be stable, predictable, and emotionally gentle, then you may need to ask yourself if this space is for you.

The vertical world right now belongs to the mavericks, the hustlers, the builders, and the creators who are willing to go into the trenches and get their stories made even when there is no roadmap.

As for me, I love it. I love my job. I love the creativity, the speed, the chaos, the problem-solving, and the satisfaction of seeing a story come to life in real time. Even when it is frustrating, even when I am exhausted, I would not want to do anything else.

TAKE ACTION: STEP 25

Never start without a signed contract

- Vet producers
- Negotiate fair payment terms
- Set boundaries on revisions
- Save part of every payment
- Stay active in vertical communities

You're not just writing a script. You're building a *career*.

CHAPTER 26
PITCHING YOUR SERIES
TURN YOUR STORY INTO THEIR OBSESSION

THE ONE-PAGER THAT SELLS

You have written your script. Now you need to pitch your next one. Producers rarely hire writers who only have one idea. They hire writers who feel like a slate. Writers who can say, "I have romance, thriller, horror, melodrama. What do you need?"

This chapter is about building your arsenal. You are creating a bank of high-concept pitches organized by genre, ready to send the moment a producer asks, "What else do you have?"

WHY YOU NEED MULTIPLE PITCHES

The reality: most producers will not hire you based on a single concept.

They will ask:

- Do you have romance?
- Do you have something darker?
- Any thrillers?

If you say, "Just this one," the conversation will probably end.

If you say, "I have 15 concepts across romance, thriller, melodrama, and horror. Which genre interests you most?" you become valuable.

The goal: 10-20 pitches ready to go.

WHAT YOU ACTUALLY NEED

You need:

- 20 to 30 one-page pitches, organized by genre
- 10-episode writing samples in 2 or 3 genres

You do not need:

- A full 60-episode script for every idea
- Fully developed outlines for all 20 concepts

This is a writer-for-hire market, not a spec script market. Producers are not usually buying your finished scripts. They are hiring you to write their concepts, or they are choosing from your concepts to develop together.

YOUR WRITING SAMPLE PORTFOLIO

Minimum portfolio:

2 to 3 completed 10-episode samples (12 to 18 pages each) in different genres.

For example:

- 10 episodes of a romance
- 10 episodes of a thriller
- 10 episodes of a melodrama

Why 10 episodes and not 60?

10 episodes prove that:

- You understand vertical structure
- You can write cliffhangers
- You can hook viewers in Episode 1
- You can build toward an Episode 10 paywall hook

If they like your 10 episodes and your concept, they will hire you to write the full 60.

What About Your Full 60-Episode Script?

Use it as your primary master sample. It shows you can deliver a complete series. You do not need to write 60 episodes for every concept you pitch.

THE PITCH PACKAGE SYSTEM

Organize your pitches by genre.

For example:

- **Romance**: 10 concepts
- **Thriller**: 7 concepts
- **Melodrama**: 5 concepts
- **Horror**: 5 concepts

When a producer says, "I am looking for romance," you send your romance list. When they say, "Got any thrillers?" you send your thriller list. You are not scrambling to invent ideas on the spot. You are prepared.

THE ONE-PAGE PITCH FORMAT

Each concept gets exactly one page.

Format:

Title: Clickbait

Genre: Genre

Episodes: 60

LOGLINE: [PROTAGONIST] must [GOAL] or [STAKES], but [OBSTACLE] plus [TWIST].

SYNOPSIS (One Paragraph): Three to five sentences that cover the setup, complication, core conflict, and emotional stakes. Do not include the full resolution. Leave them wanting more.

CHARACTERS:

Protagonist: Name, age, occupation. Two to three sentences about wound, goal, and arc.

Antagonist or Love Interest: Name, age, occupation. Two to three sentences about their role in the story.

Key Supporting Characters: Two or three characters with one to two sentences each.

WHY THIS WORKS COMMERCIALLY:

- Proven genre or trope
- Built-in conflict
- High re-watchability
- Clear audience or demographic appeal

VISUAL (Optional but powerful): One AI-generated poster or mood image that fits the concept

Total length: One page.

EXAMPLE ONE-PAGE PITCH

THE BLIND BRIDE OF THE SCARRED MAFIA BOSS

Genre: Romance, Mafia

Episodes: 60

Comparables: Peaky Blinders meets Bridgerton

LOGLINE: (this one was provided by the client) A blind mafia heiress goes undercover in a rival family to solve her brother's murder, but when she falls for their son, the man she is supposed to destroy, she must choose between love and revenge.

SYNOPSIS: Eleanor Battisti is not actually blind. She is pretending so she can infiltrate the Romano family and avenge her brother's death. Forced into a political marriage with Alexander Romano, the scarred heir haunted by guilt, she discovers he is not the monster her family claimed. As attraction turns into obsession and then real vulnerability, each of them must decide what is worth more, loyalty to family or the chance at love that could destroy everything.

CHARACTERS:

Eleanor Battisti, 26, undercover operative. Pretends to be blind to infiltrate the enemy family. Wound: Raised as a weapon.

Goal: Avenge her brother while keeping her heart guarded. Arc: From powerless pawn to powerful queen.

Alexander Romano, 32, mafia heir. Scarred and guilt-ridden. Wound: Convinced he is a monster who does not deserve love.

Goal: Keep his family alive and his past buried. Arc: From guilt and self-hatred to acceptance and redemption.

Lorenzo De Palma, 35, advisor. Loyal to Alexander, suspicious of Eleanor. Torn between duty, jealousy, and his own secrets.

WHY THIS WORKS COMMERCIALLY:

- Enemies to lovers and marriage of convenience, both proven romance tropes
- Secret identity and fake blindness create instant intrigue
- Mafia romance is a high-performing vertical genre

- Built for female-gaze intimacy and emotional cliffhangers every 10 episodes

Visual: An elegant woman in a wedding dress with a blindfold, a scarred man in a suit behind her, a mansion in the background, dark romantic lighting.

CREATING YOUR CONCEPT POSTERS

Use AI image tools to create one compelling visual for each pitch.

Tools you can use:

- Midjourney
- Nano Banana
- Leonardo AI
- ChatGPT

Why it helps:

- Shows you are serious
- Makes each concept more memorable
- Helps producers visualize the show
- Elevates your presentation
- Looks great in decks and on Zoom calls

Design principles:

- Clean, not cluttered
- High-quality images only
- Mood and color palette that match the genre
- Easy to read on a phone screen

ORGANIZING YOUR PITCH LISTS

Romance List (10 Concepts)

Create a file with 10 one-page romance pitches:

- The Blind Bride of the Scarred Mafia Boss
- [Concept 2]
- [Concept 3]
- [Concept 4]
- [Concept 5]
- [Concept 6]
- [Concept 7]
- [Concept 8]
- [Concept 9]
- [Concept 10]

Do the same for other genres:

- Thriller List: 7 concepts
- Melodrama List: 5 concepts
- Horror List: 5 concepts

File naming:

- YourName_RomanceConcepts.pdf
- YourName_ThrillerConcepts.pdf
- YourName_MelodramaConcepts.pdf
- YourName_HorrorConcepts.pdf

YOUR WRITING SAMPLE STRATEGY

1. Write your first complete 60-episode script.
2. Extract the first 10 episodes as a sample.
3. Write additional 10-episode samples in 2 other genres.

Now you have:

- One complete 60-episode series (proof you can finish)
- Three 10-episode samples in three genres (proof of range)

When pitching you can say:

- Here is my complete series in [Genre A].
- I also have 10-episode samples in [Genre B] and [Genre C].
- And I have 20 more concepts ready to develop.

That is the difference between "I wrote a script" and "I am a writer you can build a slate with."

TAILORING YOUR PITCHES

Premium or prestige producers: Send more elevated concepts with strong themes and sophisticated premises.

Commercial or platform producers: Send high-concept, hooky ideas with proven tropes and clear emotional engines.

International producers: Send concepts that travel well. Less cultural specificity, more universal emotions and situations.

Always think: Who is my audience on the producer side, and what fits their slate?

THE PITCH EMAIL

When a producer says, "What else do you have?" you answer quickly and clearly.

Example:

Hi [Producer Name],

Great question. I have 20 plus vertical series concepts across multiple genres. Which genre interests you most? I have:

- 10 romance concepts
- 7 thriller concepts
- 5 melodrama concepts
- 5 horror concepts

I also have completed 10-episode writing samples in romance, thriller, and melodrama to demonstrate my range. Happy to send whichever fits your slate.

Best,

[Your Name]

They tell you the genre. You send that PDF immediately.

TRACKING YOUR PITCHES

You must track who you pitched and what you sent. Memory is not enough. Create a pitch tracking spreadsheet.

Columns:

- Producer name
- Company
- Email or contact
- Date pitched
- Concepts pitched
- Writing samples sent
- Response (interested, passed, no response)
- Follow-up date
- Status
- Notes

Why this matters:

- You do not pitch the same concept to the same producer twice
- You know when to follow up

- You see which concepts get the best response
- You have a record in case of disputes
- Use Google Sheets so you can access it from anywhere.
- Add this line to every pitch email:

These concepts are proprietary and cannot be used without a signed agreement.

It does not guarantee protection, but it is better than nothing.

THE PITCH DECK (OPTIONAL BUT POWERFUL)

For bigger meetings or premium producers, build a simple deck.

Format: Canva offers the best pitch deck options now. Or Keynote, Google Slides or PowerPoint.

Structure:

Title Slide: Your name, "Vertical Series Concepts," contact info.

Who You Are: Two or three sentences about your vertical experience and why you are qualified.

Concept Slides (one per slide):

- Title
- Logline
- Comparables
- Characters
- Synopsis
- Tone and style

Next Steps:

"Let us discuss which concepts resonate."

"I can deliver an outline in three days and a full script in ten days after outline approval."

Visual presentation:

- Each concept visually distinct
- Mood-appropriate images
- Clean layout
- Large fonts for phone viewing

WHEN TO USE WHICH FORMAT

One-page PDFs: Quick email responses, "What else do you have?" messages.

Pitch deck: Zoom meetings, formal pitches, festival or market meetings.

Logline list only: Casual networking, DMs, social media.

10-episode samples: When they want proof of your writing before hiring.

Full 60-episode script: When they want assurance that you can complete a series.

THE PITCH MEETING

When you get a pitch meeting:

Phase 1: Warm them up (5 minutes)

- Do not start by unloading 20 concepts.
- First, frame the opportunity of vertical series:
- The size and growth of the market
- Lower production costs
- Fast turnaround
- How it fits their brand or audience
- Make them excited about the space itself.

Phase 2: Ask questions

- What type of stories are you most interested in right now?
- What does your slate look like?

- Are there specific platforms or audiences you are targeting?

Listen for genuine excitement. That is your guide.

Phase 3: Pitch focused concepts

- Once you know the genre they care about, pitch 3 to 5 loglines in that genre.
- Watch their reactions. When you hit the concept that makes them lean in, stop pitching new ones and stay with that idea.

Phase 4: Move to next steps

End with something like:

"I can have a detailed outline to you in three days and a full script ten days after you approve the outline. What are your next steps?"

You always want clarity on what happens after the meeting.

COMMON MISTAKES

- Only having one concept
- Pitching all 20 ideas at once
- Being overly attached to a single idea
- Pitching without any visuals
- Using vague, generic loglines
- Not tracking who you pitched what to
- Converting a feature script just by chopping it up.
- Writing full 60-episode scripts for every concept before talking to anyone
- Do not sink months into writing six full scripts when one strong full series and several tight one-pagers will do the job.

BUILDING YOUR PORTFOLIO

Suggested pace:

Month 1:

- Create 5 concepts across 2 genres (10 total).
- Complete your first 60-episode script.

- **Month 2:**
- Add 5 more concepts.
- Write a 10-episode sample in a second genre.

Month 3:

- Reach 20 to 30 concepts across at least 3 or 4 genres.
- Write a 10-episode sample in a third genre.

Ongoing:

- Watch which concepts get traction
- Retire ideas that never land
- Replace them with stronger, fresher concepts

Your portfolio should evolve with the market and with your own growth.

THE REALITY CHECK

Not every concept will sell. You might pitch 20 concepts before one moves forward. That is normal.

The writers who succeed are not the ones with one perfect idea. They are the ones with a pipeline.

One "yes" can lead to multiple projects with the same producer if you keep refilling that pipeline.

UPDATING YOUR PITCHES

Every few months:

- Remove pitches that never get interest
- Add 5 new ones
- Refresh visuals
- Explore new genres or sub-genres
- Update any market notes if you include them

Think of your concept library as a living catalogue.

TAKE ACTION: STEP 26

1. Create 10 one-page pitches across 2 or 3 genres.
2. Each pitch includes: Clickbait title, genre, logline, one-paragraph synopsis, character breakdown, and commercial reasons why it works.
3. Use AI tools to generate a concept image for each pitch.
4. Organize your pitches by genre into separate PDFs.
5. Write 10-episode samples in 2 or 3 genres to show range.
6. Create a pitch tracking spreadsheet with: Producer, company, date, concepts pitched, samples sent, response, follow up date, and status.

This is your arsenal. Build it now so when opportunity knocks, you are ready.

CHAPTER 27

CASE STUDY: THE BLIND BRIDE OF THE SCARRED MAFIA BOSS

STEAL MY PLAYBOOK AND DO IT BETTER

This chapter walks you through a real vertical series I wrote from start to finish, from the initial client brief to the locked script. You'll see how everything you've learned in this book applies in practice: The creative decisions, the outlining process, the revisions, and what it actually looks like to deliver a vertical series under pressure. This is proof that the method works.

FROM CLIENT BRIEF TO LOCKED SCRIPT

THE PROMPT I RECEIVED

Date: April 17, 2025

From: Producer

Subject: New Project – *Blind Desire* (mafia romance)

THE BRIEF:

LOGLINE: Behind masks of lies and family legacies, a scarred mafia heir and a young woman pretending to be blind are forced into a political marriage. What begins as a strategic alliance slowly turns into an irresistible attraction.

MAIN CHARACTERS:

Alexander Romano: Scarred mafia heir, known for ruthlessness, hiding guilt over his friend's death.

Eleanor Battisti: Rival family's daughter, pretends to be blind but sees everything, sent to infiltrate and destroy.

Lorenzo De Palma: Alexander's trusted advisor, suspicious of Eleanor from day one.

CORE PREMISE: Two mafia families at war. Forced marriage to seal truce. Two people hiding who they really are. Desire becomes obsession becomes vulnerability.

TONE: Dark, intimate, seductive. *Peaky Blinders* meets *Bridgerton* with a mafia twist.

REQUIREMENTS:

- 60 episodes / 90 pages
- Episode 3: Establish relationship
- Episode 5: Establish conflict
- Episode 10: Paywall hook
- Cliffhangers every episode (especially 1–30)
- Intimate scenes, female gaze
- Open to light comedy moments

TIMELINE: A five-week delivery schedule.

A TIGHT TIMELINE + AN EVEN TIGHTER TRAVEL SCHEDULE

"Since I'll be in Europe from May 12 through June 5, I need to deliver the script before I leave. If the notes arrive on schedule, I can fast-track the

entire process." The plan was to finish the entire series before my trip and hand in the locked script early.

But then–

The notes were delayed.

And suddenly, finishing early became impossible.

I left for Europe on May 12. First stop: **The International Cannes Film Festival.**

I had hoped to walk into Cannes with the outline approved and the draft underway.

Instead:

- Notes were delayed
- Approvals lagged
- I was stuck waiting for feedback I desperately needed
- My writing window evaporated

So I had no choice but to **write the majority of the script while traveling through Europe:** trains, hotel rooms, cafés, airports. Two days in Spain became my only real stretch of uninterrupted writing, and I used them to power through the final episodes.

This was one of the most difficult deliveries of my career.

"BEHIND THE MASK OF LIES AND FAMILY LEGACIES"

That single line became the thematic backbone of the entire series.

Every major character wears a mask:

- **Eleanor**: Pretends blindness, hides mission, conceals feelings
- **Alexander**: Projects ruthlessness, hides mercy, conceals guilt
- **Lorenzo**: Presents loyalty, hides jealousy
- **Luca**: Protective father facade, hides monstrous manipulation

- **Serena**: Dutiful daughter, hides fears and doubts

Whenever I was stuck, I asked myself:

Whose mask is cracking in this episode?

It gave the series cohesion.

ROMEO & JULIET MEETS MR. & MRS. SMITH

The moment I read the brief, I saw the structure:

Warring families → *Romeo and Juliet*

Married spies with secrets → *Mr. & Mrs. Smith*

The synthesis worked perfectly for vertical format.

The central question: *Can love survive the truth?*

- Episodes 1–20: Build the lie
- Episodes 21–44: The lie unravels
- Episodes 45–60: Can love survive once masks fall?

THE OUTLINE: 60 EPISODES OF CONTROLLED CHAOS

The outline included:

- Title, logline, thematic statement
- Character bios
- 60 episodes with 4–5 lines each
- Cliffhangers labeled clearly

This outline became my safety net, especially since I was writing while traveling.

THE MAJOR CHANGE: ELIMINATING UNCLE GINO

Initially Gino was a full antagonist but notes made it clear:

- Too many villains
- Too much confusion
- Too expensive to cast another recurring role
- Luca wasn't scary enough

So I cut Gino entirely and assigned all his story weight to Luca.

Result: Luca became a terrifying, complex main villain, and the show got stronger.

THE REVISIONS: THREE ROUNDS OF NOTES

Round 1: Producer Notes

Production-related:

- Reduce night scenes
- Consolidate locations
- Add lighter moments
- Simplify medallion subplot
- Make Lorenzo sympathetic earlier

Round 2: Director Notes

- Dialogue too long → break into shorter exchanges
- Clarify blindness performance cues
- Strengthen dinner scene blocking

Round 3: Client Notes

- More romance Episodes 15–20
- Ending too abrupt → expand final episodes

- Stronger cliffhanger needed after Episode 30
- Even with the chaos, most notes were production-related, not story notes.

Why? Because the outline was strong and approved before scripting.

THE DELIVERY

Despite the delays and the travel: **Delivered one week late** due to the delayed notes.

Locked script delivered in late May. It was brutal. But I pulled it off.

WHAT HAPPENED NEXT

The series was released on Vigloo under the title:

THE BLIND BRIDE OF THE SCARRED MAFIA BOSS

And then:

- It climbed to **#1 on the platform**
- It stayed in the **top four for six straight weeks**
- As of finishing this book, it is still trending at **#4**

Vigloo doesn't share their numbers so I don't know what they looked like but I'm happy with the experience.

A vertical series written under intense pressure ended up becoming a hit.

MY THOUGHTS ON THE FINAL SHOW

I was genuinely happy with the chemistry between the actors, they brought the emotional core to life beautifully.

The director did an excellent job with the budget and schedule they had. Shooting a period-adjacent mafia romance with action, emotion, and intimacy in a tight window is extremely hard, and she delivered something atmospheric, stylish, and compelling.

Do I wish the love scenes had been a little longer?

Of course. But as you'll soon learn, or may already know, writers have **zero control** over the final product.

You write the blueprint. They build the house.

Sometimes it looks exactly like you imagined. Sometimes it doesn't. But overall? I'm very happy with how *The Blind Bride* turned out.

If you watch it, I'd genuinely love to hear what you think. **Drop me a note. :)**

WHY THIS CASE STUDY MATTERS

Because it proves the method works **in the real world** - even with late notes, travel, no time, and production constraints.

The structure held. The thematic spine held. The character arcs held.

And the show succeeded. That's what matters.

TAKE ACTION: STEP 27

1. Watch *The Blind Bride of the Scarred Mafia Boss* on Vigloo.
2. Study the structure, pacing, cliffhangers, and character arcs.
3. See how this process translates to screen.
4. Then apply the same method to your own vertical series.

You have the tools. You have the example. Now go write your own vertical series.

CHAPTER 28
YOUR VERTICAL FUTURE

ONE LAST THING BEFORE YOU GO CONQUER THE WORLD

A door is now open. Walk through it. You've read the book. You've taken the steps. You understand the format. You know the structure. You have the tools. Now comes the only question that matters:

What will you do tomorrow?

YOUR 10-DAY CHALLENGE STARTS TOMORROW

The Commitment

Tomorrow morning, you will start writing your first vertical series.

Not "someday."

Not "when I'm ready."

You will start tomorrow!

- **Day 1–2:** Concept and outline (Chapters 6–12)
- **Day 3–9:** Write 60 episodes (Chapters 13–18)
- **Day 10:** Polish and deliver (Chapter 18)

By Day 10, you will have one of the following depending on your speed:

Either a full 60-episode series or a strong 10-episode writing sample.

Both are industry-ready. Both prove you can do this.

And I'll say this clearly: I believe in you. I'm proud of you. And I know you can do this.

WHAT HAPPENS AFTER DAY 10

You now have a completed project, either a 10-episode sample or a full 60-episode script.

Now take immediate action:

1. Apply to 20 jobs.

Use your new script as your sample. Show producers you can deliver.

2. Pitch 10 producers.

Send your loglines list. Offer to write for them. Use your script as proof.

3. Start Outlining Script #2.

Momentum is everything. Your next script begins **Day 11.**

Here's the truth:

Within 30 days, you could have your first paid gig.

Within 90 days, you could have 1–3 credits.

This is not an exaggeration. This is exactly what happens to writers who show up, execute, and deliver.

But only if you get started.

NOW GO WRITE SOMETHING AMAZING

Your first script won't be perfect. You'll make mistakes. You'll learn by doing. You'll cringe at your early work later.

Good. That's growth. That's momentum. That's how every working writer begins.

Every successful vertical writer started here:

- Zero credits
- Unsure they could do it
- They started anyway.

Now they have 1, 5, 10, 20+ credits. **Why not you?**

WHAT'S POSSIBLE

Let me tell you what's possible if you start tomorrow:

30 days from now: You could have your first paid job.

90 days from now: You could have produced credits.

This industry moves fast. And it rewards writers who move with it.

This can be you.

THE FINAL CHALLENGE

Close this book. Open Final Draft. Write **EPISODE 1** at the top of the page. And begin. Don't wait for perfect. Don't wait to feel ready. Don't wait for permission. The vertical format is exploding. The opportunity is right now. The window will not stay open forever.

You have everything you need:

- Structure
- Process
- Tools
- Templates
- Career strategy

You don't need anything else. You just need to start.

MY PROMISE TO YOU

If you do the work:

- Write your script in 10 days
- Apply to 50 opportunities
- Network consistently
- Deliver high-quality work
- Stay professional
- Keep writing and improving
- Build your portfolio over 6–12 months

You will get hired. You will build a career. You will pay your bills writing.

I promise you this. But I can't do the work for you. Only you can show up.

THE LAST THING I'LL SAY

A few years from now, someone will ask you:

"How did you break in?" And you'll remember this moment, the moment you finished this book. The moment you chose: To start… or to wait. Writers who start tomorrow will shape this industry. Writers who wait will still be waiting. **Which writer are you?** Go. Write something amazing.

Your vertical future starts now.

Thank you for letting me guide you. Until we meet again!

— **Iz**

P. S. If you need a bit more help, or when you sell your first script, please reach out. I genuinely want to hear from you.

hello@21dayscreenplay.com

CHAPTER 29
THE WRITER'S TOOLKIT
GET THAT THING

Because your journey doesn't end when you close this book.

You've now learned the full system. You understand the format, the structure, the momentum, and the business behind vertical storytelling. But you don't have to do it alone. If you want extra support, accountability, or deeper training, here are your next steps.

THE VERTICAL WRITER'S TOOLKIT

Inside **The 10-Day Vertical Series Workbook**, you'll get the full step-by-step process to actually *build* your vertical series. It includes the daily 10-day roadmap, concept worksheets, episode outline templates, writing trackers, cliffhanger maps, pacing checks, submission checklists, character worksheets, location/budget trackers, and the full structure you need to write all 60 episodes from start to finish.

To access the writer's tool kit, download the workbook here: 21dayscreenplay.com/bookbonuses

BOOK CLUB & WRITING GROUP GUIDE

Use these discussion prompts to deepen your understanding of the vertical format, spark creative exploration, and support one another as you build your series. Whether you're meeting in person, on Zoom, or inside a writers' group, these questions will help you go further, think bigger, and write smarter.

DISCUSSION QUESTIONS

1. **How do you see vertical microdramas reshaping storytelling?** Explore how they're changing pacing, structure, and character engagement.
2. **Which popular genre or trope could be reimagined for the vertical format, and how would you make it feel fresh?** Think popular tropes, but heightened for 60–90 second chapters.
3. **What's your creative process for finding a strong hook or great story idea?** Compare methods. Share where your best ideas come from.
4. **How do you write characters that resonate?** Discuss tricks that help audiences care in under 30 seconds.
5. **Share a great cliffhanger you've seen in a vertical microdrama.** What made it effective? How can you replicate that kind of tension?
6. **What are ways to surprise viewers without relying on clichés or shock-for-shock's-sake twists?** Talk about originality in a fast-paced format.
7. **What genre mashup would you love to explore in the vertical space?** Fun combinations encouraged.
8. **What's your next creative goal?** Challenge each other, set intentions, share ambitions.
9. **Practice pitching with your writing group.** Read each other's loglines, scripts, or episode samples. Give constructive feedback.

10. **How can you challenge yourself in the next week, month, and year?** Write down your goals. Make a plan. Share it for accountability. Celebrate your progress and results.

TRAIN WITH ME: YOUR NEXT STEPS

If this book opened your eyes to the possibilities of vertical storytelling, I have three ways to take you even further.

Every single one is designed to help you write better, faster, and smarter in the format that is changing our industry.

1. Start with the Free Webinar

If you want the crash course, simple, fast, and totally free, start here.

FREE 40-minute training on how to create binge-worthy vertical series

You will learn:

- What a vertical series really is
- Why this format is exploding
- What platforms like ReelShort and DramaBox expect
- How the episodic structure works
- How to position yourself so producers say yes

Sign up here:　21dayscreenplay.com

Perfect if you're curious and want a fast introduction.

2. Join the Masterclass: HOW TO WRITE A VERTICAL SERIES IN 10 DAYS

This is the deep dive. The on-demand experience. The "let me walk you through every moving part so you can actually do this" training.

In this 4-hour masterclass, you will learn how to:

- Break down what a vertical series is and why it's booming

- Understand format expectations for ReelShort, DramaBox, and more
- Structure 60–90 addictive episodes
- Build emotional hooks, cliffhangers, and momentum
- Write for low-budget, high-impact production
- Choose the right genre and concept
- Understand what gets skipped versus what gets binged
- Pitch your series to producers and platforms
- Get ahead of the curve with real industry insight

Use code **BOOK50** for **50 percent off**   21dayscreenplay.com

3. The Vertical Incubator (Limited Spots)

This is for writers who want accountability, coaching, and results.

In just **two weekends**, you will:

- Build a pitch-ready concept
- Outline 50 high-impact episodes
- Write your first 10 episodes
- Get direct feedback from me
- Learn what producers *actually* want
- Work inside a fast-moving, high-velocity environment
- Follow the exact system I used to get produced

This program sells out quickly. Check the next available date here: 21dayscreenplay.com

4. Private Consultation

If you want one-on-one guidance, personalized notes, or help developing your concept, you can book a private session here:

isabeldrean.com/consulting

Whether you want help strengthening your script, breaking a concept, getting ready to pitch, or building your vertical writing career, I've got you.

No matter how you choose to continue, I'm rooting for you.

Verticals are the new frontier. They reward bold writers, fast thinkers, and creators who can move with the times.

If that's you, welcome. Can't wait to see what you'll do.

CONTINUE YOUR JOURNEY

If you want deeper support, whether you need script feedback, concept development, or help breaking into the industry, you can always reach out.

hello@21dayscreenplay.com

I'm here for you. Thank you for reading.

-Iz

CHAPTER 30
THE MICRODRAMA PLATFORMS

WHO'S GOING TO BE THE NETFLIX OF VERTICALS? THE RACE IS ON!

THERE ARE NOW OVER 400 MICRODRAMA AND VERTICAL SERIES APPS worldwide, and the landscape is evolving at lightning speed. New platforms launch every day, often copying whatever was number one last week. The following list reflects the most active and widely used platforms as of now, but expect constant movement because this is one of the fastest changing ecosystems in entertainment.

- ReelShort
- DramaBox
- MyDrama
- VIGLOO
- AltaTV
- CandyJar
- DramaShorts
- FlareFlow
- DramaWave
- ShortMax
- NetShort
- GoodShort
- FlickReels
- MoboReels

- Kuku TV
- Playlet
- Kalos TV
- ShortsWave
- JoyReels
- DreameShort
- OneShort
- StarShort
- MiniShorts

For the full list of platforms: 21dayscreenplay.com/bookbonuses

ABOUT THE AUTHOR
PLEASE INDULGE
ME FOR A MINUTE

ISABEL DRÉAN

Isabel Dréan is a screenwriter, director, producer, and digital storytelling pioneer based in Los Angeles. Her career began in horror and psychological thrillers before an unexpected pivot into Christmas movies, a shift that transformed her trajectory, leading to five films produced in just eighteen months.

Her produced credits include *Secret Santa*, *Christmas Beneath the Stars*, *Christmas on the Rocks*, *The Holiday Swap*, and *An Eclectic Christmas*. She now teaches the popular masterclass *How to Write a Christmas Movie in 21 Days*, helping writers craft fast, marketable holiday films using her proven system.

Long before the rise of vertical entertainment, Isabel was already innovating. She created and curated her own webseries platform, developing more than fifty original shows and selling her murder-mystery series to a studio, years before *Quibi* and the global microdrama boom. Her reputation as a digital visionary was built on her ability to merge new formats with commercial storytelling.

Today, Isabel is considered one of the leading voices in vertical series. She writes, teaches, and consults internationally, guiding writers, producers, and studios through the rapidly expanding microdrama marketplace. Her vertical series **The Blind Bride of the Scarred Mafia Boss** debuted at #1 on **Vigloo** and trending for more than six weeks, solidifying her place as a creator who understands both structure and audience behavior.

She is also the founder of **THE HUB**, a curated global network onWhatsApp connecting filmmakers, producers, and financiers, responsible for multiple shopping agreements, co-productions, and career-changing collaborations.

Isabel continues to develop features, series, and vertical projects across genres, championing bold concepts and empowering the next generation of writers to build sustainable careers in a rapidly evolving industry.

To find out more, visit: isabeldrean.com

To join THE HUB - Verticals: isabeldrean.com/verticalhub

A Special Thank You

I want to take a moment to thank my editor, **Octavia McKenzie,** because none of this book would exist without her.

Octavia is the one who said, *"We've got to get your expertise into the world,"* and then rolled up her sleeves and helped me make it happen. She pushed, shaped, sharpened, and elevated every chapter. She believed in this project before I did, and I am endlessly grateful for her clarity, her commitment, and her brilliance.

She is also entering the world of vertical writing, and trust me, she is one to watch. If you are someone looking to hire writers who understand story, structure, and voice on a deep level, make sure you check her out. Thank you, Octavia. Truly.

OCTAVIA MCKENZIE (EDITOR)

Octavia McKenzie is a Brit & an American living in London. She has one son, a thousand books, and a Jane Austen obsession. She roams the West End theatre scene and loves 80s and 90s rom coms. She's a wanderlust traveler, writing screenplays, novels, and vertical dramas in her office – a coffee shop somewhere in Europe. Reach out to her here: 21dayscreenplay.com/octavia

ACKNOWLEDGEMENTS

This book was developed after teaching multiple webinars, delivering a four-hour masterclass, and running two intensive incubators. The vertical space is evolving at lightning speed. Formats shift. Markets change. Platforms move fast. I will try to update it regularly but if something becomes outdated in six months, please forgive me. Don't hold it against me. The goal is to keep you ahead of the curve, not behind it.

Thanks in advance to everyone who is reading, supporting and spreading the word about this book.

Thanks to Donna Barker for her expert guidance in the launch of this book. Here's her website: http://donnabarker.com . I highly recommend her. She's the best.

Important Note on Results and Examples

Every writer's experience and results will be different. The examples, strategies, workflows, and case studies in this book are illustrative only. They are designed to help you understand how vertical series development works, not to guarantee any specific outcome, job, financial result, or level of success. Your progress will depend on your own work, time, effort, and circumstances. Nothing in these pages should be interpreted as a promise, guarantee, or assurance of results.

instagram.com/isabeldrean
facebook.com/idrean
tiktok.com/@isabeldrean